From Creation to Resurrection

A Spiritual Journey

Sister Constance Joanna Gefvert,
SSJD

Illustrations by
Sister Mary Katherine MacDonald, SSJD

Anglican Book Centre
Toronto, Canada

1990
Anglican Book Centre
600 Jarvis Street
Toronto, Ontario
Canada M4Y 2J6

Copyright © 1990 Anglican Book Centre

All rights reserved. No part of this book may be reproduced, stored in a retrieval system, or transmitted, in any form or by any means, electronic, mechanical photocopying, recording, or otherwise, without the written permission of the Anglican Book Centre.

Scripture quotations are from *Hearing the Word: An Inclusive-Language Liturgical Lectionary* prepared by St. Stephen and the Incarnation Episcopal Church in Washington, D.C., and are used with permission.

The collects and quotations from the psalms and canticles are based on those in *The Book of Alternative Services* of the Anglican Church of Canada © 1985 by the General Synod of the Anglican Church of Canada and are used with permission.

Typesetting by Jay Tee Graphics Ltd.

Canadian Cataloguing in Publication Data

Gefvert, Constance J.
  From creation to resurrection

ISBN 0-921846-26-6

1. Easter – Meditations. 2. Bible. O.T. – Meditations. I. Title.

BV55.G44 1990   242'.36   C90-093836-6

*For my sisters and other companions
on the journey.*

Happy are the people whose strength is in you!
    whose hearts are set on the pilgrims' way.
(Psalm 84.4)

God of pilgrims, teach us to recognize your dwelling-place in the love, generosity, and support of those with whom we share our journey, and help us to worship you in our response to those who need our care; for all the world is your temple and every human heart is a sign of your presence, made known to us in Jesus Christ our Lord.[1]

WITH GREAT *tenderness*
I WILL BRING YOU HOME AGAIN

WITH ENDURING *love*
I WILL HAVE COMPASSION ON YOU

Isa. 54

Contents

Preface and Acknowledgements 1
Introduction 4
Suggestions for Using This Book 10

1 The Story of Creation 15

2 The Flood 25

3 Abraham's Sacrifice of Isaac 35

4 Israel's Deliverance at the Red Sea 45

5 The Renewal of God's Marriage to Israel 59

6 Salvation Offered Freely to All 67

7 Cling to Wisdom and Live 77

8 A New Heart and a New Spirit 85

9 The Valley of Dry Bones 95

10 The Gathering of God's People 103

Epilogue 111
A Note on the Great Vigil of Easter, Saturday Vigil, and Baptism 115
Additional Reading 120

Preface and Acknowledgements

The Great Vigil of Easter, which comes down to us from the church of the second century, carries us through an exciting journey from creation to resurrection. It begins with the lighting of the new light, symbolizing Christ's resurrection and our salvation. Then follows a kind of flashback, in which we listen to readings from the Old Testament that relate the marvelous drama of God's creation and redemption of Israel, before we progress to Baptism and the celebration of the resurrection Eucharist.

Most parishes that celebrate the Great Vigil do not use all ten readings in the Old Testament cycle, simply because they take up so much time. But in the early church, the Great Vigil of Easter was an all-night celebration in which each of the readings (sometimes as many as twelve) was savoured and meditated upon.

No matter how many readings might be used, the one which is always included, because it is pivotal, is the story of Exodus. The history of God's saving acts is most dramatically and decisively displayed in that reading, and it becomes a major metaphor for the Resurrection.

A few years ago, one of my sisters suggested that these readings provided wonderful material for personal meditation on our own individual Exodus journeys. I spent a good part of Lent that year using those ten readings, meditating on them, praying with them, and journaling about them, to help me see where God was leading me on my own journey. I found the process helpful and encouraging. Because it is so easy for us to get bogged down in the difficulties of our Christian journey, it is important to see how God uses each step of the way to bring us, gradually but insistently, out of our own personal slaveries and into a new resurrection life.

Because the meditations were so helpful for me personally, I decided, the following year, to use the Old Testament cycle from the Easter Vigil as the basis for a Lenten retreat, and over the next couple of years I used it, with variations, for a number of retreats and quiet days. I am very grateful to all the people who participated in those retreats and quiet days — for reflections shared with me and other retreatants, for questions asked and suggestions made, for wonderful poetry and other creative results. The interaction with these fellow pilgrims has deepened my own understanding of the readings and their meaning for our personal exodus journeys, the journey we each take from creation to resurrection.

Those retreat meditations, revised many times, form the basis of the reflections in this book, which I hope might be helpful for others, either individually or in parish Bible study groups or in any group of pilgrims on The Way.

I wish to thank many people who have made this book possible:

Sister Margaret Ann, who first gave me the idea of using the Easter Vigil cycle for my own meditation, who read the manuscript and made many helpful suggestions to improve it, and who has so generously and lovingly helped me on my own journey to know and love God;

Mother Frances Joyce, who has encouraged and supported me, not only in bringing this project to completion but in her loving example of what it means to walk the Christian journey;

Sister Thelma-Anne, for her reading of the manuscript and helpful suggestions, and for her encouragement and help in my work in retreats and missions.

All my sisters, for their loving support throughout my journey in SSJD, for their encouragement and prayers for this project, for filling in for many of my duties when I was given time to finish this manuscript;

Bishop Henry Hill, for his willingness to read and critique the manuscript in the midst of his own very demanding schedule, and for his very helpful criticism.

The Reverend Paul Gibson and the Reverend Victoria Matthews, who also reviewed the manuscript.

I would like to give special thanks to Sister Mary Katherine, SSJD, who did the cover art and also the calligraphy for the frontispiece and chapter openings. A few years ago, while I was preparing the first lenten retreats based on this material, she was creating a moving series of posters illustrating many of the passages from the Easter Vigil. Neither of us knew of the other's plans until I saw her completed work. It seemed to me that she had captured visually what I was trying to convey in my retreat meditations. It was an experience of grace for me to see the Word made so visible in form and light and colour. I used those posters as a focus for meditation in subsequent retreats, and they helped to deepen my own understanding of the scripture passages. While we were not able to reproduce them here, Sr. Mary Katherine has done a new series to be reproduced in black and white. As much as the earlier posters did, these illustrations powerfully convey the Word of God and remind us that the same Word proclaimed in scripture is made visible in the artistic gifts of calligraphers.

A Note on Sources

The ten readings from the Old Testament are those appointed for the Great Vigil of Easter in the Common Lectionary, an ecumenical lectionary used by the Anglican, Roman Catholic, Lutheran, and many Protestant churches.

Throughout this book I have used *Hearing the Word*[2] for all scripture quotations except the psalms and canticles, unless otherwise noted. In the few cases where a translation was not available from that liturgical lectionary, I have used the Revised Standard Version, abbreviated RSV, or *The Good News Bible*, abbreviated GNB. Where the language of the RSV or GNB is not inclusive, I have altered it to make it inclusive and have marked it *alt*.

Quotations from the psalms and canticles are based on those in *The Book of Alternative Services of the Anglican Church of Canada*, and have been edited where necessary for inclusive language.

Notes

1 *The Book of Alternative Services of the Anglican Church of Canada* (Toronto: Anglican Book Centre, 1985), p. 818.
2 *Hearing the Word: An Inclusive-Language Liturgical Lectionary* (Washington, D.C.: St. Stephen and the Incarnation Episcopal Church; Year A, 1983; Year B, 1984; Year C, 1985).

Introduction

In one of the most famous Christian classics of all times, Dante's *Divine Comedy*, the poet begins by saying,

> Midway in our life's journey, I went astray
> from the straight road and woke to find myself
> alone in a dark wood.[1]

The *Divine Comedy* continues with the dramatic and symbolic narrative of Dante's spiritual journey, from darkness and death to light and life.

Although Dante wrote around 1300, the imagery of pilgrims and journeys is millennia old — at least as old as the oral tradition behind the Hebrew scriptures. Adam and Eve started a journey the moment they were exiled from Eden, and worshippers of God since then have seen themselves as "strangers and sojourners," pilgrims who find their place in God's household (Ephesians 2.19). The Book of Exodus contains the most famous of all the journeys of the Old Testament, as the Israelites are led in a dramatic journey from slavery to freedom, only to encounter many more years of being pilgrims and sojourners in the lands of other people, and many other deliverances.

In keeping with their Hebrew background, the Christians of the first century were called people of "The Way," because they followed a spiritual path that gave meaning to the whole of their personal lives as well as their corporate lives. They saw in Jesus, as the writer of the letter to the Hebrews puts it, "the pioneer and perfecter" of their faith (12.2), the way of salvation for the whole creation.

The journey motif has continued throughout Christian literature. Dante wrote in the 13th century, but his theme is not much different from that of John Bunyan, writing *The Pilgrim's Progress* in the 17th century, or C.S. Lewis, writing the Narnia Chronicles in the 20th century. They all draw on the ancient symbolism of the journey to describe our relationship with God and our fellow creatures.

At various points in each of our lives, we awaken, like Dante, to find ourselves in the middle of a dark wood, wondering where to find the path that represents God's will for us. Sometimes this dark wood represents for us an inner forest, as we approach a turning-point in our relationship with God, in our understanding of ourselves, or in our relationships with the people we are closest to. Sometimes this dark wood seems more external, as we face some decision about career or vocation or family.

Whatever the dark wood might represent for each of us at this moment in our life's journey, we can be sure it will involve both our inner and our outer worlds. If we are facing a crossroads in our relationship with God, a call to a closer relationship with Jesus, it will affect our external life as well. If we are facing a decision in our external circumstances, it will not be authentic unless it comes from the centre of who we are as people in relation to the God who created us and redeems us.

We all experience crossroads and turns and valleys and hills in this journey of ours from birth to resurrection. And God uses all the ordinary events of our lives, the little, everyday ones as well as the big ones, to lead us along the path — if only we are open to seeing everything that happens to us as a potential means of growth. God certainly does not create all the specific events of our lives; we are free, and the people with whom we share our journey are free, to create both good and evil. But if we journey consciously with our Creator, God can use the circumstances of our lives, happy and sad, joyful and tragic, to bring us into closer union with our Lord and closer to the fulfilment of our journey.

In the following meditations, we will consider how we can be open to God's guiding us in this journey of ours, so that instead of wandering aimlessly in the woods or the desert, we find a clear footpath. The basis for the meditations are the Old Testament readings for the Easter Vigil. They are particularly meaningful during Lent as we prepare for Holy Week and Easter and follow our Lord's last journey through death to resurrection. But they are also meaningful at any time of the year. In fact, some of the same readings are traditional in the service of lessons and carols for Christmas because they focus on our salvation history.

The ten Old Testament readings form a cycle which developed

in the early Christian church as a way of telling the story of our journey from creation (birth) to resurrection.[2] On one level they recount the history of God's saving acts for Israel, as a prelude to the coming of the Messiah and the free gift of God's salvation to the whole world. On another level they represent (as they did for the Israelites and the early Christians) the personal journey each one of us undertakes.

As we reflect on each of the readings, there are several important points to keep in mind:

First: The journey of the Israelites is more than a metaphor for our own journeys; there is an intimate, spiritual connection between the two. Biologists tell us that the history of the human race is repeated in miniature in the biological history of each individual from the moment of conception. Similarly, our individual psychological, social, and spiritual histories repeat, with wonderful, individual variations, the history of human cultures. We can see in the Bible the development of humanity's understanding of God, just as our own understanding of God grows as we mature in our relationships with our Creator and those with whom we share our planet.

This notion that our personal lives reflect the life of the world and the human community is a very old one in Christian thought. Origen, a third-century father of the church, said:

> You yourself are even another little world and have within you the sun and the moon and also the stars.

As we reflect on the Easter Vigil cycle, we are constantly reminded that every step in the historical journey of humankind — from the creation of God's world to the end of the age and the final redemption of that world in Jesus — pervades our personal spiritual journeys.

The readings used at the Great Vigil of Easter highlight the most significant events in the spiritual history of the Hebrews, as they represent all of us. The creation of the world, Noah and the flood, Abraham's sacrifice, the Exodus, Ezekiel's vision of the valley of dry bones, and the other prophecies that tell of God's redemption and the coming of the Messiah — all these tell a wonderful and powerful story. It is our story, yours and mine, the story of our creation in innocence, of our separation and sin, of our repeated contrition and repentance and God's repeated forgiveness, of our repeated deaths and resurrections, and of our looking forward to our physical death and union with God in the final resurrection. As we proceed on our journeys, then, we are united with our sisters and brothers in all ages.

Second: The readings in the Easter Vigil cycle, like much of the Old Testament, are stories and prophecies; they use the language of poetry. They are not science or history, though they are based on history and though there is much history in the Old Testament. So we must listen to them and enjoy them as story — not as science — because God uses story to convey truths that cannot be expressed by science.

All our modern attempts to explain the physical universe and control it through science and technology leave the most important questions unasked: Who created the world? Who created us? Why? Why does the human race seem so flawed, so unable to reach the potential we believe we have? Why is there evil in the universe? Why have we been so unsuccessful at making ourselves good?

The answers to these questions lie in the realm of revelation, of belief and faith, not in the realm of science. However great a mystery is represented in these questions, however much they are beyond human understanding, underlying them all is the great fact of God's love, as revealed to us in God's Word — both the word of scripture and the incarnate Word, Jesus the Messiah. God created us out of pure love, and left us free. We don't understand exactly why, but we know our love would be of little value to God if we were not free to choose whether or not to love. That freedom, of course, allowed for the possibility of sin. But because we are so loved, God has worked throughout the history of humankind to redeem what we barter away. And in the end, at the consummation of the world, God promises to draw the whole creation into God's own love. As Jesus told his disciples, "when I am lifted up, I will draw all people to myself" (John 12.32).

The stories and the prophecies in the Old Testament cycle of the Easter Vigil are poetic ways of trying to convey this truth. No words of mine, or yours, or even a theologian's, can possibly explain the truth of God's love for us. But myth, story, and the poetry of prophecy can suggest it to us.

Third: What Christians know as the Old Testament is (with a few differences in the official canon) also the Hebrew Scripture. In fact, the term "Old Testament" can be misleading; while it derives from the belief that Christ embodies the "new testament" or new covenant, it can lead us to believe that the Old Testament is not meaningful for Christians, as though the law of the Old Testament were an albatross around our necks.

But Jesus said, "Do not imagine that I have come to abolish the law or the Prophets" (Matthew 5.17). Jesus is, for Christians, the culmination of God's creation, the fulfilment of the promises in the Old Testament, not the contradiction of it. As Paul said, "What the Law could not do, because human nature was weak, God did." God sent Jesus "so that the righteous demands of the Law might be satisfied in us who live according to the Spirit" (Romans 8.3-4, *GNB*).

The Old Testament was Jesus' scripture. Everything he did and said was grounded in the Hebrew religion, and must be understood in that context. The Old and New Testaments are part of one continuous revelation. Jesus is the Word of God (*Logos* in Greek) that spoke the creation into being:

> In the beginning was the Word: the Word was with God, and the Word was God. The Word was with God in the beginning, and it was through the Word that all things came into being; apart from the Word, not one thing came to be. . . . The Word became flesh and dwelt among us. And we saw the glory of the Word, such glory as befits the one and only begotten by God, full of grace and truth. (John 1.1-3, 14)

The creative love, the mercy, the justice, and the tender compassion of God, which are present supremely in Jesus, the Word incarnate, are already present at the foundation of the world and are clearly evident in the Old Testament, including the ten readings in the Easter Vigil cycle.

Therefore, we need to read these lessons not merely as historical documents, as though they were interesting for their foreshadowing but rendered insignificant by Jesus' life, death, and resurrection. Rather, we need to be aware that Jesus' life, death, and resurrection are inherent in these great stories of God's saving acts of salvation, and that they speak on a personal, intimate level to each of us.[3]

Fourth: Because of the first three points — because our personal growth is connected with that of the human race as a whole, because we are reading poetry and story, not objective history, and because the Hebrew scripture is the context in which Jesus' redeeming acts took place — we need to approach the stories in a spirit of reverent listening, in order to hear God's word as it speaks to each of us personally. The writer of the letter to the Hebrews reminds us of the immediacy and power God's word should have for us:

> God's word is living and active, and sharper than any two-edged sword. It pierces as deep as the dividing point of soul and spirit, of joints and marrow, and it discerns the thoughts and intentions of the heart. (Hebrews 4.12)

In order to let God's word speak to us, we need to listen in attentive silence. We live in a culture where words are cheap and pervasive. If the word of God in scripture is to speak to us, living and active *now*, not only as an historical document, then we need to hear it as a personal encounter with God.

As we enter into the drama of the Easter Vigil, we are invited to participate in God's history of salvation by listening and responding to these stories and prophecies. We need to listen with our hearts, and respond with our hearts. While God created our minds and gives us wonderful insights, the truths of God's love transcend the quickest and brightest of our minds. God's ultimate truth resides in our hearts. And I invite you now to reflect with me on the wonder of God's saving love — in the world, and in our personal, individual lives.

Suggestions For Using This Book

This book is designed either for individual reading and meditation or for use in a group. It would be ideal for a parish Lenten study, but could be equally useful at any time of the year when people want to think and pray about their Christian journeys.

The reflections following each reading are not in any sense meant to be a comprehensive study or biblical commentary. Rather, they represent some of the meanderings I have taken while reflecting on my own pilgrimage. Ideally they should be a stimulus for your own thinking and praying. The word of scripture is always new and has something specific and personal to say to each of us. No two people will read and respond to the scripture or the reflections in the same way, though sharing our thoughts can be helpful as we journey along the way.

If you are using this book on your own:

1 Space out your reading of the passages and reflections, and your use of the "Questions to Ponder." If you wish to use them for daily quiet time, one or two of the Vigil readings each week is sufficient, leaving you several days to meditate on each passage and to ponder some of the questions. (Take at least a week for the longer readings — especially the first four; for the others, at least half a week each.)
2 First read each of the Old Testament passages aloud to yourself, so you can *hear* God's word speaking to you as well as seeing it with your own eyes.
3 Take a few moments of quiet reflection to hear what God might be saying to *you* in that passage.
4 Read the reflections that follow the reading, along with the psalm or canticle appointed to go with it.

Suggestions for Using This Book 11

5 Again allow yourself time for peaceful reflection on the psalm or canticle, and then pray the collect that follows each reading.
6 Use the "Questions to Ponder" as a way of penetrating more deeply into the meaning the passage might have for you, personally. Use them for private prayer, and perhaps for writing in your journal.[4] Some people find they think more clearly and hear God more clearly when they write out their thoughts and prayers. Other questions and issues may also come up for you — follow wherever God's Spirit leads you.

If you are using the book with a group:

1 Take at least six to eight weeks for a discussion of these passages. A sample schedule might work out like this:

Week One:	Introduction and Reading 1
Week Two:	Reading 2
Week Three:	Reading 3
Week Four:	Reading 4
Week Five:	Readings 5 & 6
Week Six:	Reading 7
Week Seven:	Readings 8 & 9
Week Eight:	Reading 10 and Conclusion

Or

Week One:	Introduction and Reading 1
Week Two:	Readings 2 & 3
Week Three:	Reading 4
Week Four:	Readings 5 & 6
Week Five:	Readings 7 & 8
Week Six:	Readings 9 & 10

2 Read and reflect on each passage at home, as above.
3 At the meeting, have someone read the passage aloud; then together read the psalm or canticle, and the collect. Take some

time for silent reflection together. You might want to go off on your own for a few minutes, or stay silently with the group. Gently and peacefully repeat the psalm to yourself. Perhaps you will also want to reread the lesson in another translation, because that often brings about new insights. Then just let your mind gently go wherever God seems to lead you as you reflect on what the reading and psalm mean to you, personally.

If you have already pondered some of the questions yourself, at home, there will be much fruitful discussion in your sharing. If other questions come up that are more pressing in your group, don't feel obliged to discuss the questions printed here. Go wherever the Spirit is blowing in your journey together.

4 Close with a period of silent or group prayer, holding up to God the concerns that came out of your discussion. Conclude with the collect appointed for the reading and the Lord's Prayer.

A Note on Journaling

If you have never kept a journal, this would be a good time to try it. The word *journal* comes from the same root as *journey* (from Old French *jour*, meaning "day"). A journey is a daily walk on our life's path — for the Christian, a walk with God. A journal is a reflection on that journey. God gives us many gifts, and many clues about the meaning and direction of our pilgrimage. Writing down our reflections on them helps to objectify them, to stand back and see them with a fresh perspective, to get a new vision.

A journal also allows much to emerge from our unconscious into consciousness. The act of writing (like drawing or painting) is a way of releasing much that lies dormant in us. We not only come to understand things we hadn't understood before, to see patterns in what we do and what happens to us, but we also discover things about ourselves and God that we never knew.

A journal is as individual and personal as our minds and hearts.

People use journals in different ways and at different times. Some people like to keep a loose-leaf notebook, where they can write on different topics at different times. Some, for instance, keep a section for writing down dreams and reflecting on them. Dreams are a source of guidance and encouragement from God that we often overlook, and writing about them helps us to receive the gifts God gives through them.[5]

Another way of using a journal is to write down your reflections on significant happenings or conversations. A journal is not meant to be a tedious record of your daily activities, but rather an exploration of your feelings and thoughts about specific meaningful events.

One of the best uses of a journal is a kind of praying — writing down your conversations with God, especially at times when you need God's help to think clearly. Your anger, love, joy, confusion — all of these are valuable to express to God, and to hear what God may be saying to you. People often resist this kind of praying-in-writing, because they are afraid they will simply write down the confusing conversations in their own heads. Sometimes this happens, and we often have to sift out the chaff from the grain, but it is amazing how clearly we can hear God speaking to us when we write things down instead of just letting things spin out obsessively in our heads.

Writing down your reflections on scripture is also a good use of a journal. In fact, almost anything that is worth talking about with God (which is, of course, anything) is worth writing in your journal. The "Questions to Ponder" in this book will give you some good material for your journal, but so will anything of significance in your life at the moment.

Notes

1 Dante Alighieri, *The Divine Comedy*, trans. John Ciardi (New York: W.W. Norton, 1977), p. 3.
2 See Appendix for a brief description of how the Great Vigil of Easter developed in the early church.

3 It is partly for this reason that the Common Lectionary (which is the one in *The Book of Alternative Services* and the new service books of many other denominations) has restored the practice of the early church in including Old Testament readings at the Eucharist. Similarly, each of the Eucharistic prayers in the *BAS* and other new liturgies (like the liturgies of the early church) recounts the saving acts of God, culminating in Jesus, as one great story.
4 See the end of this section for some suggestions on journaling.
5 See the "Additional Reading" at the end of this book for suggestions of some books on dreams and journaling.

1
The Story of Creation

Darkness
was upon
the face of the abyss

and the Spirit of God
was brooding
over the face of the waters

Gen. 1

The Story of Creation

In the beginning God created the heavens and the earth.

The earth was a desolation and an emptiness; darkness was upon the face of the abyss, and the Spirit of God was brooding over the face of the waters. And God said, "Let there be light," and there was light. God saw that the light was good; and God separated the light from the darkness. God called the light "day" and the darkness "night." And there was evening and there was morning — the first day.

And God said, "Let there be an expanse between the waters, to separate water from water." So God made the expanse, and separated the water under the expanse from the water above it. And so it was. God called the expanse "sky." And there was evening and there was morning — the second day.

And God said, "Let the waters under the sky be gathered into one place, so that dry ground may appear." And so it was. God called the dry ground "land," and the waters that were gathered "seas." And God saw that it was good. Then God said, "Let the land produce vegetation — seed-bearing plants and trees bearing fruit with seed inside, each according to its kind." And so it was. The land produced vegetation — seed-bearing plants and trees bearing fruit with seed inside, each according to its kind. And God saw that it was good. And there was evening and there was morning — the third day.

And God said, "Let there be lights in the expanse of the sky to separate the day from the night, and let the lights serve as signs to mark seasons, days, and years; and let them also shine in the expanse of the sky to give light on the earth." And so it was. God made two great lights, the greater light to govern the day and the lesser light to govern the night, and made the stars as well. God set these lights in the expanse of the sky to give light on the earth, to govern the day and the night, and to separate light from darkness. And God saw that it was good. And there was evening and there was morning — the fourth day.

And God said, "Let the waters teem with living creatures, and let birds fly above the earth across the expanse of the sky." God then created the great creatures of the sea, and every kind of living creature that moves and swarms in the waters, and every kind of bird. And God saw that it was good. God blessed them and said, "Be fruitful, multiply, and fill the waters of the seas; and let birds multiply on the earth." And there was evening and there was morning — the fifth day.

And God said, "Let the land produce living creatures, according to their kind — domestic animals, creatures that crawl along the ground, and wild animals, all according to their kinds." And so it was. God made the wild animals, the domestic animals, and all creatures that crawl along the ground, each according to its kind. And God saw that it was good.

Then God said, "Let us make humankind in our image and likeness; and let them have dominion over the fish of the sea and the birds of the air, over the domestic animals, over all the earth, and over every creature that crawls upon the ground." In the very image of God, then, was humankind created; male and female, God created them. God blessed them and said to them, "Be fruitful and multiply; fill the earth and subdue it; and have dominion over the fish of the sea, and over the birds of the air, and over every living creature that moves upon the ground."

Then God said, "I give you every seed-bearing plant on the earth and every tree that has fruit with seed in it. They will be yours for food. And all the green plants I give for food to the wild animals, to all the birds of heaven, and all creatures that crawl upon the ground — everything that has the breath of life in it." And so it was. And God saw all that had been made, and indeed it was very good. And there was evening and there was morning — the sixth day.

Thus the heavens and the earth were completed in all their vast array. By the seventh day, God had finished all the work that was being done; so on the seventh day, God rested from all the work [of creation].

Genesis 1:1–2:2

1   Rejoice in the Lord, you righteous;
      it is good for the just to sing praises.
2   Praise the Lord with the harp;
      play to God upon the psaltery and lyre.
3   Sing for God a new song;
      sound a fanfare with all your skill upon the trumpet.
4   For the word of the Lord is right,
      and all God's works are sure.
5   God loves righteousness and justice;
      the loving-kindness of the Lord fills the whole earth.
6   By the word of the Lord were the heavens made,
      by the breath of God's mouth all the heavenly hosts.
7   God gathers up the waters of the ocean as in a water-skin
      and stores up the depths of the sea.
8   Let all the earth fear the Lord;
      let all who dwell in the world stand in awe of God.
9   For the Lord spoke, and it came to pass;
      God commanded, and it stood fast.
10 The Lord brings the will of the nations to naught;
      God thwarts the designs of the peoples.
11 But the Lord's will stands fast for ever,
      and the designs of God's heart from age to age.
12 Happy is the nation whose God is the Lord!
      happy the people chosen for God's own!
13 The Lord looks down from heaven,
      and beholds all the people in the world.
14 From the heavenly throne God's gaze is turned
      on all who dwell on the earth.
15 The Lord fashions all the hearts of them
      and understands all their works.
16 There is no ruler that can be saved by a mighty army;
      a strong person is not delivered by great strength.
17 The horse is a vain hope for deliverance;
      for all its strength it cannot save.
18 Behold, the eye of the Lord is upon those who fear God,
      on those who wait upon God's love.

19 To pluck their lives from death,
    and to feed them in time of famine.
20 Our soul waits for the Lord,
    who is our help and our shield.
21 Indeed, our heart rejoices in the Lord,
    for in God's holy name we put our trust.
22 Let your loving-kindness, O Lord, be upon us,
    as we have put our trust in you.

Psalm 33

Almighty and eternal God,
you created all things in wonderful beauty and order.
Help us now to perceive
how still more wonderful is the new creation,
by which in the fullness of time
you redeemed your people
through the sacrifice of our Passover, Jesus Christ,
who lives and reigns for ever and ever. Amen.

Collect (BAS page 325)

Reflections

In the tradition of fairy tales, many of the best stories we know begin "once upon a time," in a distantly remembered and unspecified past. But the Bible begins at a specific, determined time — in the beginning. In the beginning of all things was God, creating the universe. In the beginning of each of our lives is God, the unseen presence at our conception. And in the beginning of each new venture in our lives, each turning-point, God is there re-creating us, bringing us to birth yet one more time.

In the beginning, God created the universe. Whatever else the seven days might mean, they remind us that God's creation is orderly and sequential. One thing happens at a time. Creation and growth don't happen all at once. God must have been infinitely patient at the beginning of the world. We must be infinitely patient with ourselves and with our fellow human beings.

In the beginning, "the Spirit of God was brooding over the face of the waters." Before anything was created, there was water and the Spirit (John 3.5). We are born from the waters of the womb and we are born again through the waters of baptism. Both for creation and for re-creation we need the water of birth and the Spirit of God — the wind of God — moving over the waters.[1]

On the first day, God created light and separated it from darkness. God was pleased and "saw that it was good." On the second day, God created the sky — the expanse (or "firmament" in some translations) that separates the waters above and below the earth. The image of the expanse conveys the truth that God created this earth as a home for us that is set apart from heaven and the rest of the universe. God is both the loving creator who intimately dwells with us, and the ruler of a universe that is greater than our earth. The expanse of sky both separates and protects, a fact we are becoming tragically aware of as our irresponsible use of chemical substances has begun to erode the ozone layer that protects earth from the sun.

On each subsequent day, God continued to separate and define the earth — with the separation of land and seas on the third day; the creation of the sun, moon, and stars on the fourth day; the creation of sea creatures and birds on the fifth day; the creation of land animals and human beings on the sixth day.

With each step in this orderly creation, God designed all things to suit and help each other. God created the lights of the heaven to mark festivals and seasons for human culture and for animal life. God gave the fruit of the earth and the products of the sea to human beings for food, and God gave the green plants to animals, sea creatures, and birds. God created an order of responsibility on earth by making humanity caretakers of the creation, to be stewards of all, with an understanding of the interrelatedness of the whole creation. And God saw to perpetuating this wonderful creation by telling all living things to increase and multiply, and by providing the means for that increase to take place. In creating humanity male and female, God's wonderful economy ensured that the increase of the species would be encouraged by the gift of sexual love.

"God saw that it was good" is a refrain repeated throughout the creation story. And at the end of the seven days, when all this creating was done, "God saw all that had been made, and indeed it was very good."

What does all this say to us?

We are part of the carefully designed order God created, made in God's image and for God's purpose. That means we are "very good." However much we may be oppressed with a sense of our personal failings or the collective sinfulness of humanity, God said the creation (including each one of us) was good. And since the creation is ongoing, God surely considers each of us "very good." Everything God creates is very good, and when it goes wrong, it is redeemable. We need to value ourselves as God values us because we are made very good and we are redeemed, ultimately through the incarnation of Christ.

Everything in creation is under our stewardship, and that of course includes ourselves because we are also part of the creation. We must exercise care for ourselves and each other, as well as for the rest of creation.

God has blessed us and said "be fruitful" — that is, imitate God's loving, joyful, and creative activity. We are all given gifts to share in the ongoing creation — the gift of children, the gift of art, music, and crafts, the gift of helping people in various ways — and many other gifts to be used for the benefit of ourselves and our fellow human beings. "Each one of us," Paul says, "has received a special gift," and the purpose of those gifts is "to prepare all God's people for the work of Christian service, in order to build up the body of Christ" (Ephesians 4.7, 12).

If we use God's world with sensitivity to the needs of all God's creatures, there is nothing in the universe that can hurt us. This is hard to believe in an age when the very survival of the human race, of the earth itself, seems to be at stake. Like Frankenstein we seem to have created monsters that we cannot control, and we seem doomed to destroy ourselves with radiation poisoning if nuclear war doesn't do it first. But God has promised that the whole earth is under divine control, and responsible stewardship means co-operating with that purpose. We must pray for peace, work for peace in any way possible, pray for and work for the relief of hunger and poverty and oppression around the world. If God has made us the stewards of creation, then we must believe that God will provide the means as well, if only we are open to see. As Psalm 33 puts it,

> Behold, the eye of the Lord is upon those who fear God,
>   on those who wait upon God's love,
> To pluck their lives from death,
>   and to feed them in time of famine.

The psalm reminds us that what God makes is made to last. There is no obsolescence in God's economy. No matter how hopeless we might feel when faced with the potential destruction of our planet by pollution, rape of our natural resources, or nuclear fallout, no matter how hopeless we feel about our own imperfections and compulsions and sins, we can be confident that God's designs will be brought to perfection if we co-operate:

> For I am convinced that neither death nor life, angels nor principalities, the present nor the future, nor any powers, neither height nor depth, nor anything else in all creation, will be able to separate us from the love of God in Christ Jesus our Lord. (Romans 8.38–39)

Questions to Ponder

1 The wonderful cosmic joy that must have been experienced at the birth of the world is similar, on a more personal level, to the joy a mother experiences when she brings a child into the world. What do you remember hearing about your own birth? There is always trauma and pain at a birth, both for the mother and the child. Depending on the circumstances, some births are more traumatic than others. It is often helpful to go back in prayer to the moment of your birth and ask God to heal painful memories that you may not even be aware of.[2]

2 Go back through your life and jot down three lists:
   a experiences that you could say "it was good" to, and for which you could immediately thank God.
   b experiences that seemed painful at the time but for which you could give thanks later.
   c experiences that seem only painful still; ask God to show you how these might have within them the seeds of some learning or growing for which you may be able to give thanks later if not now.

3 How does Psalm 33 reflect on the economy of God's creation (the absence of obsolescence — things made to last)? How does it offer hope in the face of pollution, rape of our natural resources, nuclear fallout?

4 Think about verses 10-11 of this psalm. How do these verses fit in a psalm of praise of God's creation, a rejoicing in God's plan for us?

5 How can this psalm be a source of hope to us in relation to our own failings as individuals? Consider also the collect for this reading.

6 Read and ponder these passages on gifts: Ephesians 4.1-16 and 1 Corinthians 12. What specific gifts has God given you? How are you using them? How does recognition and use of our gifts help to bring unity to the church and to all creation? How can we help our fellow pilgrims recognize and use their gifts?

Notes

1 Words provide interesting clues to connections between the material and spiritual worlds. For instance, the same word means both "wind" and "spirit" in Hebrew (*ruach*) and Greek (*pneuma*).
2 See the section on Additional Reading at the end of this book for some books that deal with inner healing.

2
The Flood

I hereby establish a covenant with you and with your descendants after you and with every living creature that was with you   Gen. 7

The Flood

Yahweh said to Noah, "Go aboard the ark [you have built] — you and all your household — for I have found that you alone are righteous among this generation. Take with you seven pairs, male and female, of all the animals that are ritually clean, and one pair, male and female, of all animals that are not clean; also take seven pairs, male and female, of every kind of bird — to keep their kinds alive throughout the earth. For in seven days I will send rain over the earth for forty days and forty nights, and I will wipe from the face of the earth every living creature that I have made."

And Noah did just as Yahweh had commanded. In the six-hundredth year of Noah's life, on the seventeenth day of the second month — on that day, all the springs of the great abyss broke through, and the floodgates of the heavens were opened. And rain fell upon the earth for forty days and forty nights. On the very day [that the rains began], Noah and his wife boarded the ark together with their three sons (Shem, Ham and Japheth) and their three daughters-in-law. They had with them wild animals of every kind, domestic animals of every kind, creatures of every kind that crawl upon the ground, and winged birds of every kind. They all went into the ark with Noah — one pair of all creatures in which there was the breath of life. And so there entered a male and female of every creature that is flesh, just as God had commanded Noah. Then Yahweh closed the door of the ark on Noah.

The flood continued upon the earth for forty days. The waters swelled and lifted the ark high above the earth. The waters rose and swelled greatly on the earth; and the ark floated on the surface of the water. After forty days, Noah opened the window he had made in the ark and sent out a raven, which flew to and fro until the waters dried up from the earth. Then Noah sent out a dove, to see if the waters were receding from the surface of the land. But because there was yet water over the whole surface of the earth, the dove found nowhere to perch, and so she returned to Noah in the ark. Putting out his hand, he took hold of her and brought her back into the ark with him. Noah waited another seven days, and again sent out the dove from the ark. In the evening, she came back to him with a freshly plucked olive branch in her beak. Then Noah knew that the water had receded from the earth. He waited seven more days and released the dove again; but this time she did not return to the ark.

By the first day of the first month of Noah's six-hundred-and-first year, the water had dried up from the earth. Noah lifted the hatch and looked out of the ark: the surface of the ground was dry. By the twenty-seventh day of the second month, the earth was completely dry. Then God said to Noah, "Come out of the ark — you and your wife, your sons and your daughters-in-law. Bring out every kind of living creature that is with you — the birds, the animals, and all the creatures that crawl upon the ground — so they can swarm over the earth, and be fruitful and multiply there." So Noah and his wife came out, together with their sons and daughters-in-law.

Then God said to [the family], "I hereby establish a covenant with you, and with your descendants after you, and with every living creature that was with you — the birds, the domestic and wild animals — with everything that came out of the ark with you, with everything that lives on the earth. And this is the covenant I will maintain with you: never again will all life be cut off by the waters of a flood, never again will a flood destroy all the earth."

And God said, "Here is the sign of the covenant I am making between me and you (and every living creature with you), a covenant for all generations to come. I have set my rainbow in the clouds, and it will be the sign of the covenant between me and the earth."

Genesis 7:1–5, 11–18; 8:6–18; 9:8–13

The Flood

1 God is our refuge and strength,
   a very present help in trouble.
2 Therefore we will not fear, though the earth be moved,
   and though the mountains be toppled into the
   depths of the sea;
3 Though its waters rage and foam,
   and though the mountains tremble at its tumult.
4 The Lord of hosts is with us;
   the God of Jacob is our stronghold.
5 There is a river whose streams make glad the city of God,
   the holy habitation of the Most High.
6 God is in its midst;
   it shall not be overthrown;
   God shall help at the break of day.
7 The nations make much ado, and the kingdoms are shaken;
   God has spoken, and the earth shall melt away.
8 The Lord of hosts is with us;
   the God of Jacob is our stronghold.
9 Come now and look upon the works of the Lord,
   what awesome things God has done on earth.
10 It is the Lord who makes war to cease in all the world;
   God breaks the bow, and shatters the spear,
   and burns the shields with fire.
11 "Be still, then, and know that I am God;
   I will be exalted among the nations;
   I will be exlated in the earth."
12 The Lord of hosts is with us;
   the God of Jacob is our stronghold.

Psalm 46

Faithful God,
you have placed the rainbow in the skies
as the sign of your covenant with all living things.

May we who are saved through water and the Spirit,
worthily offer to you our sacrifice of thanksgiving.
We ask this in the name of Jesus Christ our Lord. Amen.

Collect (BAS page 326)

Reflections

In Genesis 1 we read the story of how the world was created. In Genesis 6—9, the story of Noah and the flood, we learn how the world was *re*-created. Water plays a central role in both stories. The first parallels our own birth; the second parallels our baptism and all the other rebirths we experience in our lives. "The Spirit of God was brooding over the face of the waters" (Genesis 1.2). Just as the world was created out of water, so each of us begins life in a sac of water, in our mother's womb; and just as in the story of Noah the world is re-created through water, so we are re-created through the symbolic washing of baptism.

The re-creation is necessary because almost immediately after the creation of the world and the first man and woman, we learn of the entrance of sin into the universe, and we learn that humanity gradually became more and more corrupt, until God had to perform a major cleansing project.

The early books of Genesis are not meant to give a philosophical or theological explanation of why sin and evil exist; rather they try, through myth and story, to present the essential truth of human morality: that we were created with free will (how else would there be any meaning to our lives?), and that we choose, over and over, the wrong thing. The story of Adam and Eve being tempted in the garden is not an explanation of *why* or *how* sin came into the world, except in the general sense that we human beings are responsible because we *choose* to be disobedient. Likewise, the story of Noah and the flood is not an explanation of *how* God forgives and cleanses us, but rather a way of showing, through myth and story, that God does offer us the option of repentance and forgiveness and rebirth.

We are told that Noah is the only person on earth who "does what is right," that is to keep God's covenant (the law, the Word) by which God created the world and formed it into an order, with a plan for all of God's creatures.

But as we saw in Psalm 33 (vv 10–11), the others devised their own plans and were destroyed. It took one good human being, or rather one good human family, to save the earth, in a story that prefigures the death and resurrection of Jesus. Unlike Jesus, Noah did not have literally to die and be reborn. But the year[1] Noah and his family spent in the ark is a symbolic death. Noah was closed up in a tomb-like (or womb-like) ark, and floated on the waters of the flood. Inside the ark with Noah was all manner of life and activity, reminding us that what goes on in each of us leads to life, just as the life that slowly grows in a mother's womb is in fact a vital, active life from the moment of conception until the moment of birth. And we must infer that new life was constantly being created within the womb of the ark, for Noah was able to send out many birds.

The story of Nicodemus (John 3.1–8) is a good illustration of how important rebirth is. When Nicodemus comes to question Jesus at night, Jesus tells him he must be born anew. Nicodemus is astounded: "One certainly can't go back into a mother's womb to be born a second time!" (John 3.4). But Jesus insists; "unless you are born of water and the Spirit, you cannot enter the kingdom of God" (John 3.5). Our first birth is in water. Our second birth, our baptism, is of water and the spirit.

The Spirit of God brooded over the waters in the beginning of creation, and the dove (a symbol of the Holy Spirit) which Noah sent out of the ark comes back finally to testify to the moment of birth, when there is no water left to brood over and the dry land again appears. And the Spirit of God broods within us to bring us to new birth, perhaps many times during our lives.

The rebirth in this story is a *universal* rebirth — all the creatures and plants that God put in subjection under humans are now under humans again: a restoration of the order and harmony of creation. The rainbow suggests a circle, connecting all of life under it with the earth. The rainbow is also reminiscent of the "firmament" that God used to separate heavens and earth at creation. Its refraction of light reminds us that the source of life is God, "the light of life," through whom life itself is reflected in the great diversity yet harmony of creation.

What practical meaning does all of this have for our personal lives? First, God promises never again to destroy the earth with water. We can participate in that promise by trusting and believing that we are part of that creation, and doing whatever we can to help bring it about. This means engaging in practical prayer and action — praying for peace, for instance, or working in some concrete way to help bring about peace — but it also means an inner attitude of openness to God's plans, in all the big and little events of our lives.

Every time we try to control our destinies by creating our own order and trying to shape our personal universes, we end up in confusion and even chaos. The only way to be free from the bondage of compulsive control — by groups or by individuals — is to trust in God's plan and God's protection of us, not our own protection of ourselves.

God's promise is never again to destroy the earth with water. But there may be other kinds of destructions we need to face, both personally and corporately, in order to fulfil God's creation. Sometimes we are freed from one bondage only to become aware of another. We may, with each attempt to enter into God's will (symbolized by God's ark), move toward further liberation. We are in the process of *being* reborn. As Paul says, "I die every day" (1 Cor. 15.31, RSV), and every day we are also reborn.

We need never fear death to self, to self-preservation, to self-ordering — it will always lead to rebirth. As the collect says, the rainbow is a sign of the covenant through which we are saved by water and Spirit — death and rebirth.

Questions to Ponder

1 What moments of re-birth or re-creation have you experienced in your life? What dark woods, or womb-like periods have you gone through when all seemed dark but was followed by the birth of some new understanding or new relationship (with yourself, God, others)?

2 Write a description of some of the dark woods, deserts, or womb-like environments you have found yourself in. Are some periods like a woods (dark and moist, with much light and shadow, teeming with chaotic life — perhaps more like a jungle)? Some more like a desert (dry and bright but with no apparent sign of life or nourishment)? Some more like a womb (cosy and comfortable but not very energetic)?

3 Were the births out of each of these periods traumatic? Or a relief? Or both? What new life emerged in you and around you after each of these periods?

4 How does Psalm 46 comment on our attitude to experiences of death and rebirth? Consider especially verses 1–2.

5 How are we saved "through water and the Spirit"? Consider the collect for this reading.

6 The last chapter of Isaiah has a beautiful and hopeful image of God helping Jerusalem (which symbolizes the people of God) to be reborn. Read Isaiah 66.7–14, and consider how it applies to you, personally, as belonging to the spiritual Jerusalem, and how it applies to the Christian church.

Notes

1 As the story is told in the "Priestly" source of Genesis, the rain started on "the six-hundredth year of Noah's life, on the seventeenth day of the second month" (Genesis 7.11); the earth was dry enough for Noah and his family to leave the ark "by the twenty-seventh day of the second month" of Noah's six-hundred-and-first year (Genesis 8.14).

3
Abraham's Sacrifice of Isaac

I WILL BLESS YOU ABUNDANTLY AND MAKE YOUR DESCENDANTS AS MANY

as the stars of heaven

and as the grains of sand on the seashore

Gen. 22

Abraham's Sacrifice of Isaac

It came to pass that God tested Abraham. God called "Abraham!" and he replied, "Here I am." Then God said, "Take your only child, your son Isaac whom you love, and go to the region of Moriah, and sacrifice him there as a burnt offering on one of the mountains which I will show you."

So Abraham rose early the next morning, saddled his donkey, and took with him two servants and his son Isaac. When Abraham had cut enough wood for the burnt offering, he set out for the place of which God had spoken. On the third day, Abraham looked up and saw the place in the distance. He said to the servants, "Stay here with the donkey, while the boy and I go over there; and when we have worshiped, we will come back to you." Abraham took the wood for the burnt offering, laid it on the shoulder of his son Isaac, and carried in his own hands the fire and the knife. Then the two of them set out together.

"Father?" Isaac said to Abraham.

"What is it, my son?" Abraham answered.

Isaac said, "The fire and the wood are here, but where is the lamb for the burnt offering?"

Abraham answered, "It is God who will provide the lamb for the burnt offering, my son."

And the two of them went on together. When they reached the place of which God had spoken, Abraham built an altar there and arranged the wood on it. Then he bound his son Isaac and laid him on the wood on the altar. Then Abraham reached out his hand and took the knife to kill his son. But the angel of Yahweh called out from heaven, "Abraham! Abraham!"

He answered, "Here I am."

The angel of Yahweh said, "Do not raise your hand against the boy; do not harm him. For now I know that you have a holy fear of God, because you have not withheld from God your son, your only child."

Abraham looked up, and there in the thicket he saw a ram caught by its horns. So he went over and took the ram and offered it as a sacrifice instead of his son. So Abraham called the place

"Yahweh provides." And to this day there is a saying: "On the mountain of Yahweh, it is provided."

The angel of Yahweh called from heaven to Abraham a second time, and said, "I swear by my own self — it is Yahweh who speaks — that because you have done this, because you have not refused me your only child, your son, I will bless you abundantly and make your descendants as many as the stars of heaven and as the grains of sand on the seashore. Your descendants shall take possession of the cities of their enemies; and through your offspring, all nations on earth shall be blessed — because you have obeyed me."

Genesis 22:1–18

1. Protect me, O God, for I take refuge in you;
   I have said to the Lord, "You are my Lord,
   my good above all other."
2. All my delight is upon the godly that are in the land,
   upon those who are noble among the people.
3. But those who run after other gods
   shall have their troubles multiplied.
4. Their libations of blood I will not offer,
   nor take the names of their gods upon my lips.
5. O Lord, you are my portion and my cup;
   it is you who uphold my lot.
6. My boundaries enclose a pleasant land;
   indeed, I have a goodly heritage.
7. I will bless the Lord who gives me counsel;
   my heart teaches me, night after night.
8. I have set the Lord always before me,
   my God who is at my right hand.
9. My heart, therefore, is glad, and my spirit rejoices;
   my body also shall rest in hope.
10. For you will not abandon me to the grave,
    nor let your holy one see the Pit.

11 You will show me the path of life;
   in your presence there is fullness of joy,
   and in your right hand are pleasures for evermore.

Psalm 16

God and Father of all who believe in you,
you promised Abraham
that he would become the father of all nations,
and through the death and resurrection of Christ
you fulfil that promise;
everywhere throughout the world
you increase your chosen people.
May we respond to your call by joyfully accepting
your invitation to the new life of grace.
Grant this through Christ our Lord. Amen.

Collect (BAS page 326)

Reflections

Have you ever wondered what Isaac said or how he reacted when Abraham bound him up? Did Abraham explain, and did Isaac accept the explanation? Or did Isaac know intuitively that in some mysterious way this was part of God's plan, and that he must follow it? The obedience that a son owed a father in ancient Israel was absolute, and so Isaac may never have questioned. In any case, he surely must have gone through a powerful death-and-rebirth experience. To have the knife of sacrifice raised above him, and then to be saved at the last minute — that must have been like a resurrection.

And what of Sarah? Did she know what Abraham and Isaac were about that morning when they set out on their journeys?

How did she feel? What must she have had to sacrifice in order to let her only son, a miraculous gift from God, go off to seeming death?

The major focus in this story, however, is on Abraham, and his sacrifice. Abraham must have gone through a death-and-rebirth experience no less powerful than Isaac's.

In such a significant human drama it is frustrating at first to think we're told so little about the feelings and reactions of the central characters. But sometimes what we are *not* told in a story helps us focus on what the writer considers really important.

We're told that "God tested Abraham." So we know that this whole event is under God's control. This seems like a terrible testing, even a cruel one. Abraham and Sarah had become used to having no children, and then when they were very old, God promised them a child and promised that their descendants "will become a great and mighty nation" and that through them, "I will bless all the nations" (Genesis 18.18 GNB). It was such a preposterous notion that Abraham had difficulty believing it (much as Zechariah did when God told him that Elizabeth would bear John the Baptist). Abraham and Sarah even laughed, it seemed so hard to believe. And they tried to take matters into their own hands by having a child by Sarah's servant, Hagar. They simply couldn't believe that God could make Sarah pregnant by Abraham.

But the wonderful miracle really did happen, and Sarah bore Isaac. Then it must have seemed a cruel God who would set Abraham and Sarah up for such a terrible disappointment. They might have wondered why God ever gave them the child to begin with. But so far as we know, they never questioned God's goodness.

And by the end of the story, we realize what God is asking. God asks Abraham to put God ahead of everything — even ahead of the son he loves so much. And when Abraham obeys, God provides a divinely arranged sacrifice in place of Isaac. Not only that — God promises to bless all the descendants that will come through Isaac — "because you have obeyed me," God says to Abraham.

So the very sacrifice Abraham is asked to make, and emotionally does make, becomes the source of blessing from God.

We also learn some important things in this story about what Abraham is like. Each time God speaks to him Abraham says, "Here I am" — or else he just does what God says without commenting. And when Isaac asks him where the lamb is for the burnt offering, Abraham simply says God will provide. Abraham has very little to say in this story, but he is a person who above all *listens* and *obeys*.

There are some important implications in this story for us.

First, isn't it amazing that Abraham says so little in such difficult circumstances? What if we just said "Yes, here I am" each time God asked us to take some new leap of faith? The word *obedience* comes from a Latin word (*obedire*) that means both "to listen" and "to respond." Like Noah, Abraham listened. And he obeyed. Adam and Eve did not obey and, we might wonder, were they really listening?

God asks Abraham to sacrifice "your only child, your son Isaac whom you love" (Genesis 22.2). Maybe Abraham had his own plans and ideas about how Isaac was to fulfil God's promise, and God had to ask him to sacrifice those so he could be open to *God's* plans.

In this, Jesus is our great model and enabler. Jesus had to endure rejection, suffering, and death. His total obedience and abandonment to God not only show us the way, but also provide the grace we need to follow that route of self-forgetfulness and self-abandonment.

We are often asked to sacrifice whatever hinders our journeys with God — our plans for ourselves — and all the fears, useless anxieties, compulsions, self-will, hurts, and resentments that come when we try to follow our ways instead of God's. If we are to be part of the *order* of creation, to be part of the self-giving, self-sacrificing way of God and God's people, then sacrifice — dying to ourselves, to everything that we hold more dear than God — is the way. Jesus said:

You are not worthy of me if you do not take up your cross and follow me. For if you find your life, you will lose it; and if you lose your life, for my sake, you will find it." (Matthew 10.38-39)

God promises Abraham that all nations will be blessed through Isaac, and so we have a renewal of the covenant that was broken in the Garden of Eden. The history of salvation is a history of covenants made and broken — the covenant made at creation when human beings were made stewards of creation; the covenant made with Noah after the flood; and the covenant renewed here, when God promises Abraham that "through your offspring, all nations on earth shall be blessed — because you have obeyed me" (Genesis 22.18).

The collect that follows this reading says, "everywhere throughout the world you increase your chosen people." In each lesson so far, "increase and multiply" has followed upon obedience and a recognition of God's goodness. We too must have the faith that our obedience to God's will for us will bring blessings. And then perhaps we will be able to say "yes" joyfully, not with the reluctance or resentment that is so often born of fear. And then we will "increase and multiply" in the gifts God had given us to share with others.

Questions to Ponder

1 When have you felt God was asking you to sacrifice something that seemed very painful to let go of at the time, but which, after you had offered it up, turned out not to be a sacrifice but a gift?

2 Rewrite this story from Sarah's point of view or from Isaac's point of view. How does it help you understand better your own relationship with God?

Abraham's Sacrifice of Isaac   43

3 How does Psalm 16 form a commentary on this story? Consider especially verses 7–10.

4 When have you felt abandoned to the grave, as Isaac must have felt? How did God rescue you? What was your response? Consider also the collect for this reading.

5 The end of Psalm 16 (verse 11) expresses the psalmist's confidence in God's guidance. Try writing a verse of your own that would express your vision of your continued walk with God in the future, based on your past experience of God's redemption.

4
Israel's Deliverance at the Red Sea

DON'T BE AFRAID
              DON'T BE AFRAID
stand firm and see the
deliverance
DON'T BE AFRAID Yahweh will bring you today
        DON'T BE AFRAID
              Ex. 14

Israel's Deliverance at the Red Sea

[With chariots and horses, cavalry and infantry, Pharaoh, king of Egypt, pursued the Israelites.] When the Israelites looked up, they saw the Egyptians were almost upon them. In terror, they clamored to Yahweh for help. And to Moses they said, "Were there no graves in Egypt, that you had to lead us out to die in this wilderness? See what you've done to us by bringing us out of Egypt! This is exactly what we meant when we said in Egypt, 'Leave us alone. Let us go on being slaves to the Egyptians. Better to work for them than to die in the wilderness!'" Moses answered the people, "Don't be afraid! Stand firm and see the deliverance Yahweh will bring you today. You will never see these Egyptians again. Yahweh will fight for you; you need only to keep still." Yahweh said to Moses, "What's the meaning of all this uproar? Tell the children of Israel to go forward. You, Moses, hold up your walking stick and stretch your hand out over the sea. Divide the water, so that the Israelites can get through the middle, walking on the seabed. For my part, I will make the Egyptians so stubborn that they will keep pursuing you. I will get honor at the expense of Pharaoh and his chariots and horses, cavalry and infantry. The Egyptians will know that I am Yahweh when I have won glory for myself over their Pharaoh and his army."

The angel of God, who had been in front of the Israelite camp, moved back to the rear. The pillar of cloud, which had been before them, also moved behind, coming between the Israelites and the Egyptians. The cloud brought on darkness and early nightfall, so the two peoples came no closer the whole night long. Moses then held his hand outstretched over the sea. All night Yahweh drove the sea back with a strong easterly wind, dividing the water and turning the seabed into dry ground. The Israelites walked through the middle, with walls of water to their right and to their left.

The Egyptians came after them — Pharaoh and his chariots and his cavalry — pursuing the Israelites far into the sea. From the pillar of fire and cloud, Yahweh looked down on the Egyptians and, just before dawn, threw them into confusion, clogging their chariot wheels so that they could hardly make any headway. The Egyptians cried out, "It is Yahweh fighting for Israel against Egypt. Let us flee!"

Then Yahweh said to Moses, "Stretch out your hand over the sea, and let the water flow back over the Egyptians, their chariots and their cavalry." Moses stretched out his hand over the sea and, as day broke, the water again covered over the seabed. Even then the Egyptians were in flight, but they were swept out into the middle of the sea by Yahweh. The returning waters overwhelmed Pharaoh's whole army, the chariots and the cavalry, which had followed the Israelites into the sea. Not a single Egyptian survived. But the Israelites walked through the sea on dry ground with walls of water to their right and to their left.

That day Yahweh saved Israel from the power of Egypt, and the Israelites saw the Egyptians lying dead on the seashore. When Israel saw the great power that had been put forth against Egypt, all the people were in awe of Yahweh. And the Israelites put their faith in Yahweh and in Moses, Yahweh's servant.

Then Miriam the prophet, who was the sister of [Moses and] Aaron, took a tambourine in her hand; and all the women followed her with tambourines and dancing. And Miriam led them in this refrain: "Sing to Yahweh, who has risen up in triumph, hurling horse and rider into the sea."

Exodus 14:10–31, 15:20–21[1]

I will sing to the Lord who has triumphed gloriously;
   the horse and the rider have been hurled into the sea.
The Lord has become my strength and refuge;
   the Lord our God has become my Saviour.

You are my God and I will praise you;
   the God of my forebears and I will exalt you.
The Lord our God is strong to save;
   the Lord, Yahweh, is God's name.

Your right hand, O Lord, is glorious in majesty;
   your right hand, O Lord, gives us strength.
Who is like you, O Lord, among the gods,
   holy, awesome, worker of wonders.

In steadfast love you led your people;
   you guided your redeemed with your great strength.
You brought them in safety to your holy place,
   and planted them firm on your own mountain.
You brought them into your own house.
   The Lord shall reign for ever and ever.

The Song of Miriam and Moses[2]

God of steadfast love,
your wonderful deeds of old shine forth even to our own
   day.
By the power of your mighty arm
you once delivered your chosen people
from slavery under Pharaoh,
to be a sign for us of the salvation of all nations
by the water of baptism.
Grant that all the peoples of the earth
may be numbered among the offspring of Abraham,
and rejoice in the inheritance of Israel.
We ask this through Jesus Christ our Lord. Amen.

Collect (BAS page 326)

Reflections

This account of God delivering the Israelites from slavery in Egypt is certainly one of the most dramatic and exciting of all the stories in the Bible, though many people find it difficult to rejoice with the Israelites because God seems so partial to them and so cruel to the Egyptians. How can we rejoice at the victory of the Israelites at such great cost to the Egyptians? The same problem has bothered rabbinical commentators, and whatever we say about this passage, however we rejoice in God's salvation of the Israelites, we must mourn the death of the Egyptians (as we must also mourn the death of all those killed in the flood when only Noah and his family were saved). One Jewish tradition from the first centuries after Christ puts it this way:

> Though we descend from those redeemed from brutal Egypt,
> And have ourselves rejoiced to see oppressors overcome,
> Yet our triumph is diminished
> By the slaughter of the foe,
> As the wine within the cup is lessened
> When we pour ten drops for the plagues upon Egypt.[3]

At the time this story was recorded, Yahweh was still seen as a tribal god, who had to prove superiority over other gods, so celebrating the death of enemies was a way of acclaiming God's power. The psalms, too, are full of references to celebrating when our enemies are killed, and it is sometimes embarrassing to read those parts of the psalms. We may feel morally superior to the biblical writers and assume that we would never feel that way about *our* enemies. We do, however, often feel that way, even if we deny or repress it. In reading those biblical passages that express joy at the destruction of enemies, we can express, and then try to transcend, that unredeemed, primitive part of ourselves that we cannot deny. But the passage above from the Passover narrative reminds us that God's compassion is far greater than our own limited view. In a world torn by war and greed and violence, we can never assume that God is on the side of any particular nation or tribe or family. God's compassion holds us all in love.

The Exodus story promises that God will redeem us — will free us from our slavery to whatever internal or external enemies are symbolized for us in the Egyptians. And it promises that we — and all the other nations upon earth — will be redeemed through

Israel. In spite of the death of the Egyptians, the real message of the Exodus is the promise of Yahweh's compassion to *all* people.

Another problem in this passage is whether or not the exodus was an historical event. Most biblical scholars agree that there was some event that freed the Israelites from bondage to the Egyptians, but the details of it belong to the oral tradition, and like all oral history, its telling would have been altered over the hundreds of years between the event (or most likely, long series of events) and its first written form.

In whatever way biblical scholars might resolve the historical problems in this passage, what is most important is that it demonstrates God's wonderful power to save. The meaning of the Exodus story lies in the symbolic power it has had for Jews and Christians throughout several millennia, and it speaks as strongly to us today.

All the drama in the story is meant to build up our reverence and gratitude to God. Try to visualize it. Thousands of Israelites, on their feet, being pursued by thousands of Egyptians "with chariots and horses, cavalry and infantry." As in many adventure stories, we have the good folk — the Israelites, very vulnerable — being pursued by the bad folk — the Egyptians, well equipped. In many adventure stories, the good side wins because virtue triumphs, because they have goodness on their side.

In this story, though, the Israelites are not represented as morally superior. In fact, right from the beginning God's people were continually disobeying God's word, and it doesn't get any better with Moses and his generation. What saves the day in this story is that God, not the Israelites, controls the events.

The Israelites grumble and complain — they are terrified and can't see how anything but death will come of this plan of God's and Moses'. But God gets Moses to calm the people down and instil confidence in God. Yahweh said to Moses, "What's the meaning of all this uproar? Tell the children of Israel to go forward" (v 15).

At that point the drama begins to increase, as we see the pillar of cloud moving behind the Israelites — a symbol of God getting in a protective stance between the Israelites and the Egyptians. And then comes the actual account of the crossing — the wind (or spirit — Hebrew *ruach* means both) of God separates the waters so the Israelites can pass through safely — reminiscent of the Spirit of God dividing the waters at creation. And this, of course, is a *new* creation.

The Israelites are like many of us when someone tells us they are doing something "good for us." We are often inclined to think that the old way is better. The Israelites complain because they're afraid:

> Were there no graves in Egypt, that you have to lead us out to die in this wilderness? . . . This is exactly what we meant when we said in Egypt, "Leave us alone. Let us go on being slaves to the Egyptians. Better to work for them than to die in the wilderness!" (vv 11–12)

This attitude is typical of most people. Somehow, somewhere deep inside, we're *afraid* to be freed from our bondage to fear, to the compulsive need to control our lives. We all experience fear and anxiety as an instinctive reaction to our birth and to circumstances in our babyhood and childhood. As we grow into adulthood and learn that we do not need to be so afraid, however, we are often unable to adjust our thinking, emotions, and external behaviour to reality, and we find it hard to give up those defensive and compulsive patterns we learn so early. We find it hard to give up that emotional and spiritual bondage for unknown (and therefore scary) freedom. What will happen to us if we let go our control and give God a chance to direct us? Will we be *killed*?

That's what the Israelites thought. But Moses tells them, "Don't be afraid! Stand firm and see the deliverance Yahweh will bring you today. . . . Yahweh will fight for you; you need only to keep still" (Exodus 14.13–14).

Yahweh will fight for us — we need only to keep still. But keeping still and waiting for God is not easy for most of us. How do we go about doing it?

I think there are three conditions for release from bondage that are illustrated in this story:

Israel's Deliverance at the Red Sea

First, to recognize our bondage and want to do something about it. The Israelites were sick and tired of being the slaves of the Egyptians and longed for freedom. But they were unable to win their own freedom, or perhaps unwilling to let go of the security of their bad situation for the unknown process of escaping into the wilderness.

And that brings us to the second condition — to recognize that only our trust in God and God's guidance can free us from our spiritual and emotional bondage.

The final condition is to be willing to let God do this, and to have the patience to let God do it *God's way*, in *God's* time — not according to our own agendas.

For those who follow God's way (as the Israelites do), the water of the Red Sea is the means to life. It is a baptism. But for those who do not (symbolized by the Egyptians), it is the means of death.

And one important thing to remember about all three of these conditions: we will, being human, fail to meet them, over and over — just as the Israelites kept backsliding through Old Testament history. But God will always, no matter what, take us back. We can be sure that God doesn't expect us to go through life without making many mistakes — the capacity to be imperfect seems to be inseparable from our having been created with freedom. What God expects of us is not perfection, but growth. Or perhaps we should say perfection is growing into what God wants us to be — it is a process, not a condition. So we can learn from each round of disobedience and complaining and grumbling, until finally we are brought to the end of our long exodus journey and see Jesus face to face.

The last verse of the canticle that follows this reading begins, "In steadfast love you led your people." It is God's steadfast, always faithful and hopeful love that guides us and brings us out of our bondage. The exodus is the beginning of the salvation history which eventually, as the collect puts it, will bring "all the peoples of the earth" to "rejoice in the inheritance of Israel." But the lesson from Exodus itself concentrates also on the individual fears and victories of those who are brought out of slavery.

It is a major metaphor for what later evolves into Christian baptism, prefigured in this dramatic event involving both the water and the spirit.

Canticle 1, The Song of Moses, as it is often called, is taken from Genesis 15.1–18 and may be an expansion of Miriam's song in Genesis 15.20–21 (or perhaps Moses was simply given credit for what Miriam composed). The version printed above is based on the canticle in the *Book of Alternative Services*[4] but has been edited for inclusive language, and has been retitled to give credit to both brother and sister. As you recite the canticle, try to imagine how the Israelites would have felt after God had given them such great liberation, and think of some liberation of your own that you can give thanks for through this song.

Questions to Ponder

1 Using a large sheet of paper, draw a "map" of your spiritual journey so far.

  a Start with a simple timeline: put on it the place you were born, the places you have lived (the highlights if you have moved a lot) and the people who were most influential at each point in your journey.

  b This is the outer "route" of your journey. Add to it the major external changes that have occurred that were most significant to you (feel free to be creative, if you want to indicate secondary roads and byways, hills and valleys, etc.).

  A few suggestions of things you might include:

  the first time you went to school
  the divorce or death and/or remarriage of parents
  the death of other important people in your life
  the first time you went away from home for any length of time
  your earliest experiences in church

Israel's Deliverance at the Red Sea 55

> your times of searching for your own religious understanding, which may have taken you away from church and formal religion
>
> your first awareness of your sexual development and encounters with the opposite sex
>
> important events in jobs or school as you grew into adolescence
>
> career and/or educational choices
>
> marriage, children, or other major changes in living patterns
>
> a major travel experience
>
> anything else that seems like a major change in your road from time to time.

c Now add to your map the *inner* changes that occurred. Many of them may be parallel to specific outer events in your life, but many will not be. What bondages have you been in and been rescued from? What bondages are you still in and need to be rescued from? Are the bondages due to external circumstances (a job that it seems you can't change, for instance, or a family responsibility you can't escape)? Or are they due to inner compulsions, fears, anxieties? Be sure to write down the rescues as well as the bondages.

d Can you see a direction in which God is leading you? Where is it obvious that you were following God's leading? Where were you going against it? How did God redeem those false by-roads and bring good out of them? How can you transfer your learning from one bondage to another, and use your own past experience to help God rescue you? This is an exercise you may want to add to as you continue throughout this book.

2 The Song of Miriam and Moses is a song of celebration by the people of Israel, based on the song that Miriam led the women in singing after they had successfully crossed the Red Sea and were in safety. Picture her, standing on the shore of the sea, with the women gathered around, singing and dancing and playing her tambourine. In Jewish tradition, the singing of this *Shirat ha-Yam* (Song of the Sea) is one of the most important moments in the liturgical year, because "the overwhelming sense of gratitude that the Children of Israel felt at the sea still reverberates in the hearts of their descendants."[5]

Now think of one specific bondage you have been in that God has rescued you from. Perhaps it was a one-time difficulty, perhaps something that has plagued you over and over. Write your own canticle, in which you praise and thank God for the bondage you have been brought out of, and express confidence in God's continuing ability to rescue and guide you. Is it possible to rejoice in your victory over enemies without rejoicing in the death of your enemies? Consider the following comment from the Talmud (a collection of commentary on the Torah dating from the second century B.C.):

> God does not rejoice at the death of sinners. On seeing the destruction of the Egyptians the angels wanted to break forth in song. But God silenced them saying: "The work of My hands is drowning in the sea, and you desire to sing songs!"[6]

3 How can we as Christians extend the exodus experience to others? Ponder the collect that follows this reading.

Notes

1. The *BAS* closes this passage with Exodus 15.1, in which Moses leads the people in the victory song. The *ILL* uses instead Exodus 15.20–21, an earlier version of the event, in which Miriam and the women sing the verses which were later expanded into the victory song attributed to Moses. For this reason, I have called the canticle based on this song "The Song of Miriam and Moses."
2. From Exodus 15.1–3, 6, 11, 13, 17–18; based on Canticle 1 in the *Book of Alternative Services*, p. 75.

3 From a Passover narrative quoted in *Wellsprings of Torah*, ed. N.L. Alpert (New York: Judaica Press, 1969), vol. 1, p. 130.
4 *Book of Alternative Services*, p. 75.
5 As quoted in W. Gunther Plaut, ed., *The Torah: A Modern Commentary*, (New York: Union of American Hebrew Congregations, 1981), p. 487.
6 As quoted in Plaut, p. 486.

5
The Renewal of God's Marriage to Israel

O storm battered city
Distressed & disconsolate
I will build you
with stones of finest mortar
and set your foundations
with sapphires   Isa. 54

The Renewal of God's Marriage to Israel

Your maker will be to you a husband whose name is Yahweh Sabaoth. Your redeemer is the Holy One of Israel, who is called God of all the earth. Yes, Yahweh calls you back as if you were a wife abandoned and heartbroken, a wife who married in youth only to be rejected.

"For a brief moment I did forsake you," says your God, "but with great tenderness I will bring you home again. For a moment, in a surge of anger, I hid my face from you; but with enduring love, I will have compassion on you," says Yahweh your redeemer. "The days recall for me the days of Noah, when I swore that the waters would never again flood the earth. So now I have sworn not to be angry with you, or to rebuke you. Though the mountains move and the hills be shaken, my love for you will be immovable and never fail, and my covenant of peace shall not be shaken." So says Yahweh, who has compassion on you.

"O storm-battered city, distressed and disconsolate, I will build you with stones in the finest mortar and set your foundations with sapphires. I will make your battlements of rubies, and your gates of crystal, and all your walls of precious jewels. Your children will all be instructed by Yahweh; and great will be your children's peace. In righteousness will you be established. You will be safe from oppression, and you will have nothing to fear. Terror will be far removed; and it will not come near you."

Isaiah 54:5-14

1 I will exalt you, O Lord,
   because you have lifted me up
      and have not let my enemies triumph over me.
2 O Lord my God, I cried out to you,
      and you restored me to health.

3   You brought me up, O Lord, from the dead;
      you restored my life as I was going down to the grave.
4   Sing to the Lord, you servants of his;
      give thanks for the remembrance of God's holiness.
5   For God's wrath endures but the twinkling of an eye,
      the Lord's favour for a lifetime.
6   Weeping may spend the night,
      but joy comes in the morning.
7   While I felt secure, I said,
      "I shall never be disturbed.
        You, Lord, with your favour, made me as strong as
          the mountains."
8   Then you hid your face,
      and I was filled with fear.
9   I cried to you, O Lord;
      I pleaded with the Lord, saying,
10 "What profit is there in my blood, if I go down to the Pit?
      will the dust praise you or declare your faithfulness?
11 Hear O Lord, and have mercy upon me;
      O Lord, be my helper."
12 You have turned my wailing into dancing;
      you have put off my sack-cloth and clothed me with joy.
13 Therefore my heart sings to you without ceasing;
      O Lord my God, I will give you thanks for ever.

Psalm 30

O God,
you led your ancient people
in a pillar of cloud by day and a pillar of fire by night.
Grant that we who serve you now on earth,
may come to the joy of that heavenly Jerusalem,
where you wipe away all tears,

The Renewal of God's Marriage to Israel

and where your saints for ever sing your praise.
Grant this through Christ our Lord. Amen.

Collect (BAS page 327)

Reflections

The Hebrew Bible is made up of three parts: the *Torah* (the first five books of the Old Testament, known in Greek as the Pentateuch), which means "law" or "teachings"; the *Nebi'im*, the "prophets" (which includes, in addition to the prophets, the historical books of Joshua, Judges, Samuel, and Kings): and the *Kethubim*, or "writings," which include the poetic and wisdom literature.

The first four readings in the Easter Vigil cycle come from the Torah. The history of humankind and of Israel are told in reference to the growing relationship between God and God's people, from the creation through the renewal of the creation after the flood, the new covenant God established with Abraham, the rescue of Israel from slavery in Egypt, and a renewed covenant.

The remainder of the readings are, with one exception,[1] taken from the Nebi'im — from prophets whom God sent both to warn the people of Israel about where their sins were leading them, and to encourage them to restore and recreate and use the nation of Israel to bring all the world into God's kingdom.

Readings 5 and 6 come from a prophet of the sixth century B.C. called Second Isaiah because his writings were incorporated in the book of Isaiah (an eighth-century prophet), and because he wrote very much in the tradition of the first Isaiah. Second Isaiah wrote around 550-538, when the Persian emperor Cyrus defeated Babylonia and made it possible for the Jewish exiles there to return to Jerusalem and rebuild the temple.

This lovely passage, full of hope, was written shortly before the Jews returned. It begins with the beautiful promise that "Your maker will be to you a husband whose name is Yahweh Sabaoth."

The great God of creation, "the Holy One of Israel," is also an intimate lover, who promises, "with deep love I will take you back" (v 7) and who will never forsake the Israelites, no matter how much they have rejected God's love.

God promises both to restore the Israelites to their homeland, and to restore the broken covenant that had led to the exile in the first place. In Genesis, when the covenant was restored between God and Noah's family, God had promised never again to destroy the earth by water; in this passage God goes further and promises never again to be angry:

> These days recall for me the days of Noah, when I swore that the waters would never again flood the earth. So now I have sworn not to be angry with you, or to rebuke you. Though the mountains move and the hills be shaken, my love for you will be immovable and never fail, and my covenant of peace shall not be shaken." So says Yahweh, who has compassion on you. (vv 9–10)

The writer of Psalm 46 also insists that our creator is more trustworthy and more enduring than the creation:

> God is our refuge and strength,
>   A very present help in trouble
> Therefore we will not fear, though the earth be moved;
>   And though the mountains topple into the depth of the sea.

No matter how much God's creation may crumble, God is greater; and no matter how far God's people may wander from obedience to God's commands, God will always take them back. And God's love will also bring about justice. As God promises to rebuild Jerusalem, out of sheer love, God also promises:

> In righteousness will you be established. You will be safe from oppression, and you will have nothing to fear. (Isaiah 55.14)

How does this relate to us?

Though we fail, over and over, in our attempts to follow God's will, like the prodigal son of Luke 14 our return to God will always be met with divine love. Remembering this should help us stop the chain reactions of guilt and self-hatred that so many of us are plagued with. "If we admit our sins, God is faithful and just, and forgives us our sins and cleanses us from all unrighteousness" (1 John 1.9). While God wants us to recognize when we have wandered from divine love and justice, and to repent of it, God longs for us to respond to that wonderful love and accept God's forgiveness, not to wallow in guilt and fear and depression. "Your maker will be to you a husband," who wants only for us to come home, that God may love us.

Questions to Ponder

1 At what points in your journey have you found yourself in exile because you have wandered away from God's path? What was the exile like? How did God rescue you? Through another person, perhaps? Through reading the Scriptures? Through a sermon or the liturgy? How did you know it was OK to come home again?

2 Consider the parable of the prodigal son in Luke 14.11–32. How does it enlighten your understanding of this passage from Isaiah?

3 How does Psalm 30 remind us that we can trust God always to help us out of bondage, to take us back when we fall — when we drift into our own plans — and to lift us to new life from the death of disobedience? Consider especially verse 10.

4 How does the collect for this reading connect the exodus with this prophecy?

Notes

1 The exception is the book of Baruch, which in some sources is part of the book of Jeremiah but which is not a canonical part of the Hebrew Bible.

6
Salvation Offered Freely to All

COME ALL YOU WHO ARE THIRSTY
COME ALL YOU WHO ARE THIRSTY
COME ALL YOU WHO ARE THIRSTY
COME ALL YOU WHO ARE THIRSTY
COME TO THE WATERS··

Isa. 65

Salvation Offered Freely to All

[Yahweh says,] "Come, all you who are thirsty, come to the waters. Come, you who have no money, buy and eat. Come, buy wine and milk — without money and without cost. Why spend money and get that which is not bread? Why spend your labor on that which does not satisfy? Listen, listen to me; and you will have good food to eat, and you will delight in the richest of fare. Give heed and come to me; listen, that you may live.

"I will make with you an everlasting covenant, the enduring love promised to David. I made him a witness to the peoples, a leader and instructor of the nations. And you, in turn, will summon nations you do not know; and those you know not will hasten to you, because Yahweh your God, the Holy One of Israel, has endowed you with glory."

Seek now, while Yahweh may yet be found. Call now, while Yahweh still is near. Let the wicked forsake their ways, and those who are evil abandon their thoughts. Let them return to Yahweh, who will have pity on them — return to our God, who will freely forgive. For Yahweh declares, "My thoughts are not your thoughts; neither are my ways your ways. As high as the heavens are above the earth, so high are my ways above your ways, and my thoughts above your thoughts. As the rain and the snow come down from heaven, and do not return until they have watered the earth — making it blossom and flourish, to give seed for sowing and bread for eating — so it is with my word. What goes forth from me will not return fruitless, but it will accomplish my purpose and achieve the end for which I sent it."

Isaiah 55.1–11

Surely, it is the Lord who saves me;
 I will trust in God and not be afraid.

For the Lord is my stronghold and my sure defence,
  and God will be my Saviour.
Therefore you shall draw water with rejoicing
  from the springs of salvation.
And on that day you shall say,
  Give thanks to the Lord and call upon God's name;
make God's deeds known among the peoples;
  see that they remember that God's name is exalted.
Sing the praises of the Lord, who has done great things,
  and this is known in all the world.
Cry aloud, inhabitants of Zion, ring out your joy,
  for the great one in the midst of you is the Holy One of Israel.

Song of Thanksgiving[1]

O God,
by the power of your Word
you have created all things,
and by your Spirit you renew the earth.
Give now the water of life to those who thirst for you,
that they may bring forth abundant fruit
in your glorious kingdom.
We ask this through Jesus Christ our Lord. Amen.

Collect (BAS page 327)

Reflections

This passage also comes from Second Isaiah, who is clearly a poet of some power and depth, as well as a prophet. He uses rhetorical questions to try to get his hearers to realize how we have drifted away from God's plans and to offer an invitation to *listen* and *respond* (the definition of obedience):

Salvation Offered Freely to All

> Why spend money and get that which is not bread?
> Why spend your labour on that which does not satisfy?
> Listen, listen to me; and you will have good food to eat.
> (Isaiah 55.2)

The listening happens through God's word in holy scripture. And that word is a creative word:

> As the rain and the snow come down from heaven,
> and do not return until they have watered the earth, . . .
> so it is with my word. What goes forth from me will not return fruitless, but it will accomplish my purpose and achieve the end for which I sent it. (Isaiah 55.10–11)

God's word continues to create, just as it did in Genesis. If we listen to that word and respond, the writer tells us, then we will bear God's fruit and will be able to assist in accomplishing the divine purpose (God's word acting in us and through us).

The history of salvation moves from the great acts of creation and redemption in Genesis and Exodus to a very personal offer of mercy and forgiveness in Second Isaiah. The food that God offers in this passage (free water, wine, and milk) prefigures both the Jewish seder meal and the Christian Eucharist. Part of the Passover Haggadah (the liturgy of the seder meal) goes like this:

> This is the bread of affliction,
> the poor bread,
> which our ancestors ate in the land of Egypt.
> Let all who are hungry come and eat.
> Let all who are in want share the hope of Passover.[2]

In the Christian Eucharist, we are offered heavenly food in the sacrifice of Jesus, the bread of life. When Jesus spoke of himself as the bread of life and the water of life, he was not just making a symbolic reference to prophecies like this one from Isaiah. Rather, he was identifying himself as the living fulfilment of the Old Testament:

I am the bread of life. Your ancestors ate the manna in the wilderness, yet they died. But this is the bread that comes down from heaven, which people may eat and not die. I am the living bread that came down from heaven. Anyone who eats this bread will live forever. This bread is my flesh, which I will give for the life of the world. (John 6.48–51)

So Jesus as the creative Word of God, and Jesus as the bread of heaven are equally rooted in the Old Testament. The bread with which we are nourished is both the word of God and the presence of Jesus in the sacrament of the Eucharist.

What practical application does this have for us?

Christians are called to speak God's word to others and to bring the bread of life to others. It is not just the preacher, the celebrant of the Eucharist, or the Christian teacher who speaks God's word. Every time one of us speaks a word of hope, of comfort, of compassion, of love to another we speak God's word. Every time we speak out for truth and justice and peace, we speak God's word. Every time we pray for the hungry, the imprisoned, the sick, the battered, the dying, we speak God's word:

What goes forth from me will not return fruitless, but it will accomplish my purpose and achieve the end for which I sent it. (Isaiah 55.11)

Likewise, we have a responsibility for the physical needs of our world as well as its spiritual needs. It does little good to pray for the hungry and starving if we are not also prepared to respond in some concrete way. In the parable of the gathering of the nations, the King says to the righteous:

Come and take your inheritance — the kingdom prepared for you since the foundation of the world. For I was hungry, and you gave me food; I was thirsty, and you gave me drink; I was naked, and you clothed me; I was a stranger, and you welcomed me; I was sick, and you cared for me; I was in prison, and you visited me. . . . whatever you did for even the most humble of my brothers and sisters, you did for me. (Matthew 25.34–36, 40)

As the passage above from the Passover Haggadah also reminds us, the free food that God promises is for everyone — the poor as well as the rich, the imprisoned as well as the free, the hungry as well as the sated. The Magnificat, the Song of Mary, is one of the great hymns of liberation in the church, reversing the values of contemporary society and reminding us that in the human community as God desires it to be, we are all responsible for each other:

> You have mercy on those who revere you
>   in every generation.
> You have shown strength with your arm,
>   scattered the proud in their conceit.
> You have brought down rulers from their rank,
>   and lifted up the lowly.
> The hungry you have filled with good things,
>   the rich you have sent away empty.
> (Luke 1.50–53)

Questions to Ponder

1 What are some of the things you have "spent money on" (either literally or figuratively) that turned out not to have the value you thought they did? How did God rescue you? What is the good food God gave you instead?

2 Consider Galatians 5.22–25 as a commentary on this passage. The Spirit of God is often identified with the Word of God, as it was in Genesis — brooding over the waters of creation. How has God's Spirit-Word brought forth fruit in your life?

3 *Canticle 3* (which comes from First Isaiah) celebrates trust in God and God's saving power. How does it help us to give thanks even for our future deliverances? Consider especially these verses:

For the Lord is my stronghold and my sure defence,
and God will become my Saviour.

4 Both Isaiah 55 and Canticle 3 talk of salvation in terms of water and the quenching of thirst:

Therefore you shall draw water with rejoicing
   from the springs of salvation.

What personal meaning do these lines have for you? Consider also the collect for this reading.

5 Psalm 62, especially verses 1–2, adds another dimension to the reading and canticle, thanking God for *continuing* to lead us out of bondage and expressing our need to have patience in waiting for God's full salvation:

For God alone my soul in silence waits;
   from God comes my salvation.
God alone is my rock and my salvation,
   my stronghold, so that I shall not be greatly shaken.

How has this passage been reflected in your own life? How might it affect you in the future?

6. Reflect on the words of the following hymn:[3]

Break thou the bread of life,
   Dear Lord, to me,
As thou didst break the loaves
   Beside the sea;

Beyond the sacred page
  I seek thee, Lord;
My spirit pants for thee,
  O living Word!

Bless thou the truth, dear Lord,
  To me, to me,
As thou didst bless the bread
  By Galilee;
Then shall all bondage cease,
  All fetters fall;
And I shall find my peace,
  My All-in-all!

Notes

1 From Isaiah 12.2–6; based on Canticle 3 in the *Book of Alternative Services*, p. 76.
2 Herbert Bronstein, ed. *A Passover Haggadah: The New Union Haggadah*, 2nd rev. ed., prepared by the Central Conference of American Rabbis (New York: Penguin Books, 1982), p. 26.
3 *The Book of Common Praise*, compiled by a committee of the General Synod of the Anglican Church of Canada (Toronto: Oxford University Press, 1938), #672.

7
Cling to Wisdom and Live

the stars shine joyfully when called they answer: "Here we are!" and gladly shine for their maker at their appointed times. Bar. 3

Cling to Wisdom and Live

Hear, O Israel, the commandments of life; listen, and learn what knowledge means. How is it, Israel, that you are in the land of your enemies, growing older and older in an alien place, sharing defilement with the dead, and reckoned with those who go to Sheol? You have forsaken the fountain of Wisdom! Had you walked in the way of God, you would have lived in peace forever. Learn where knowledge is, where strength, where understanding. Learn that, and you will know where to find life and light to walk by — long life and peace.

Who has found the place of Wisdom, who has entered her treasure house? The One who knows all knows Wisdom: she has been grasped by God's own knowledge — by the One who established the earth firmly forever and who filled it with four-footed beasts. It is God who dismisses the light and it departs, who beckons it and it obeys with trembling. The stars shine joyfully at their appointed times: when called, they answer, "Here we are!" and gladly shine for their Maker. Such is our God, to whom no other can be compared. It is God who has traced out the whole way of knowledge, confiding it to Jacob, who serves God, and to Israel, the well-beloved.

Since then has Wisdom appeared on earth, and so has she moved us. She is the book of precepts of God, the Law that endures forever. All who cling to her will live, but those who forsake her will die. Turn back, Jacob, and receive her; walk in her radiance toward light. Do not yield your glory to another, or give your privilege over to a people not your own. Blessed are we, O Israel: for what pleases God is known to us!

Baruch 3.9–15, 32—4.4

1 The heavens declare the glory of God,
and the firmament shows God's handiwork.

2 One day tells its tale to another,
   and one night imparts knowledge to another.
3 Although they have no words or language,
   and their voices are not heard.
4 Their sound has gone out into all lands,
   and their message to the ends of the world.
5 In the deep has God set a pavilion for the sun;
   it comes forth like a bridegroom out of his chamber;
   it rejoices like a champion to run its course.
6 It goes forth from the uttermost edge of the heavens
   and runs about to the end of it again;
   nothing is hidden from its burning heat.
7 The law of the Lord is perfect
     and revives the soul;
   the testimony of the Lord is sure
     and gives wisdom to the innocent.
8 The statutes of the Lord are just
     and rejoice the heart;
   the commandment of the Lord is clear
     and gives light to the eyes.
9 The fear of the Lord is clean
     and endures for ever;
   the judgements of the Lord are true
     and righteous altogether.
10 More to be desired are they than gold,
     more than much fine gold,
   sweeter far than honey,
     than honey in the comb.
11 By them also is your servant enlightened,
   and in keeping them there is great reward.
12 Who of us can tell how often we offend?
   cleanse me from my secret faults.
13 Above all, keep your servant from presumptuous sins;
   let them not get dominion over me;
     then shall I be whole and sound,
     and innocent of a great offense.

Cling to Wisdom and Live

14. Let the words of my mouth and the meditation of my
    heart be acceptable in your sight,
    O Lord, my strength and my redeemer.

Psalm 19

Creator of the universe, Source of all light,
teach us to hold fast to the ways of wisdom,
that we may live for ever in the radiance of your glory.
This we ask in the name of Jesus Christ our Saviour. Amen.

Collect (BAS page 327)

Reflections

The book of Baruch claims to have been written by the prophet Jeremiah's secretary, while the Jews were still in exile in Babylon. It was probably written much later, however, as encouragement for a persecuted nation, reflecting the destruction of Jerusalem by the Romans in A.D. 70 instead of the fall of Jerusalem to the Babylonians in the sixth century B.C. In either case, the warning is relevant that they are in the land of their enemies because they "have forsaken the fountain of Wisdom" (3.12), and the writer encourages them to seek it:

> Learn where knowledge is, where strength, where understanding. Learn that, and you will know where to find life and light to walk by — long life and peace. (Baruch 3.14)

The rest of this passage is a magnificent poem to Wisdom, which in the later Old Testament writers is identified with the Word of God and ultimately with Jesus, the Logos. In many ways, Wisdom portrays the feminine face of Jesus, and has several characteristics that are clearly identifiable with Jesus:

1 She exists from the very beginning: "she has been grasped by God's own knowledge — by the One who established the earth firmly forever" (3.32).

2 Wisdom is God's creative Word, by which God created the universe. (Baruch gives us a nutshell version of the creation story in 3.32–36.)

3 Wisdom is the totality of God's commands and law: "She is the book of the precepts of God, the law that endures forever" (4.1).

4 And Wisdom is the source of salvation: "All who cling to her will live, but those who forsake her will die" (4.1).

This poem to Wisdom is a little summary of salvation history, with a warning to the Israelites that if they don't take seriously their responsibility to bless all the nations on earth, then that responsibility will be given to others: "Do not yield your glory to another, or give your privilege over to a people not your own. Blessed are we, O Israel: for what pleases God is known to us!" (4.3–4).
   How does this relate to us?
   First, God has given us the wisdom and understanding to hear, discern, and follow God's will. But to hear in God's word the message of God's will for us is not always easy for an individual. God gives to the *community* the responsibility to discern God's will. We may have programs in mind for ourselves (as Abraham doubtless did for Isaac) that we need to put to one side before we are able to hear what *God* might intend for us.
Then listening to and really hearing the prophets, the bearers of God's will in our community, may bring wonderful surprises. As the doxology based on Ephesians 3.20 puts it,

> Now be glory to the One who is able, by the power at work within us, to do far more than we ask for or imagine.

Second, if we claim the gift of Wisdom, if we speak God's word for others, God promises it will bear fruit. As the previous reading reminds us, "what goes forth from me will not return fruitless, but it will accomplish my purpose and achieve the end for which I sent it" (Isaiah 55.11). If the Christian community is given the task of discerning God's will, then we must be bearers of God's word for each other.

Questions to Ponder

1 How does Psalm 19 connect the Word of creation (God speaking the creation into being) with the Word of the law and covenant (God speaking through scripture)? Consider especially vv 1–4.

2 In your life, how have you heard God's word most clearly — through the beauty of creation? through certain parts of scripture? through other people? Jot down some examples.

3 The collect for this reading refers to "the radiance of your glory." What meaning does that have for you in relation to the poem about Wisdom?

4 Reflect on the words of the following hymn[1]:

O Word of God Incarnate,
 O wisdom from on high,
O Truth unchanged, unchanging,
 O Light of our dark sky;
We praise thee for the radiance
 That from the hallowed page,
A lantern to our footsteps,
 Shines on from age to age.

O make thy Church, dear Saviour,
  A lamp of burnished gold
To bear before the nations
  Thy sure light as of old;
O teach thy wandering pilgrims
  By this their path to trace,
Till clouds and darkness ended,
  They see thee face to face.

Notes

1 *The Book of Common Praise*, #497, vv 1 & 4.

8
A New Heart and a New Spirit

I will give you a new heart and put a new Spirit within you

Ezek. 36

A New Heart and a New Spirit

[It is the Lord Yahweh who speaks:] "I will take you from among the nations, gather you from all the countries, and bring you home to your own land. I will pour clean water over you, and you will be clean. I will cleanse you of all your impurities and all your idols. I will give you a new heart and put a new spirit within you; I will remove the heart of stone from you and give you a heart of flesh. I will put my spirit into you, and move you to live by my laws and be careful to keep my decrees. You will live in the land I gave your ancestors. You will be my people, and I will be your God."

Ezekiel 36:24–28

1 As the deer longs for the water-brooks,
    so longs my soul for you, O God.
2 My soul is athirst for God, athirst for the living God;
    when shall I come to appear before the presence of God?
3 My tears have been my food day and night,
    while all day long they say to me,
    "Where now is your God?"
4 I pour out my soul when I think on these things:
    how I went with the multitude and led them into the house of God.
5 With the voice of praise and thanksgiving,
    among those who keep holy-day.
6 Why are you so full of heaviness, O my soul?
    and why are you so disquieted within me?
7 Put your trust in God;
    for I will yet give thanks to the Lord,
    who is the help of my countenance, and my God.
8 My soul is heavy within me;
    therefore I will remember you from the land of Jordan,

and from the peak of Mizar among the heights of
Hermon.
9 One deep calls to another in the noise of your cataracts;
all your rapids and floods have gone over me.
10 The Lord grants us loving-kindness in the daytime;
in the night season God's song is with me,
a prayer to the God of my life.
11 I will say to the God of my strength,
"Why have you forgotten me?
and why do I go so heavily while the enemy
oppresses me?"
12 While my bones are being broken,
my enemies mock me to my face;
13 All day long they mock me
and say to me, "Where now is your God?"
14 Why are you so full of heaviness, O my soul?
and why are you so disquieted within me?
15 Put your trust in God;
for I will yet give thanks to the Lord,
who is the help of my countenance, and my God.

Psalm 42

Almighty and everlasting God,
in the paschal mystery you established
the new covenant of reconciliation.
Grant that all who are born again in baptism
may show forth in their lives
what they profess by their faith.
Grant this in the name of Jesus Christ our Lord. Amen.

Collect (BAS page 328)

Reflections

The prophet Ezekiel wrote around 586, before the fall of Jerusalem. The history of Israel discloses a movement from an external covenant to an internal one, and nowhere is the internal covenant so clearly proclaimed as in Ezekiel. In Genesis and Exodus, God creates the world, recreates it, and saves the chosen nation from slavery. Over and over again, God renews the divine covenant with Israel. If you follow my commands and obey my laws, says Yahweh, I will bless you and you will be fruitful and multiply.

But the more often Israel breaks the covenant, the more obvious it becomes to the prophets that the ultimate solution must be an *inner* conversion. In this passage from Ezekiel, Yahweh promises to gather the Israelites together, to bring them home, and to restore their land. Other prophets have spoken similar words of promise and encouragement, but Ezekiel emphasizes the need for an inner renewal by the Spirit:

> I will give you a new heart and put a new spirit within you; I will remove the heart of stone from you and give you a heart of flesh. I will put my spirit into you, and move you to live by my laws and be careful to keep my decrees. (v 27)

The later prophecies of the Old Testament (during the exile, 593-571) point not only to the restoration of the Jewish nation but to a new Messianic age, in which God will intervene in the history of Israel to bring it to its fulfilment, and bring all nations to a knowledge of God. This will happen because the new covenant is an *internal* one. Jeremiah expresses the same idea in the following passage:

> "The time is coming," declares Yahweh, "when I shall make a new covenant with the House of Israel and the House of Judah. It will not be like the covenant I made with their ancestors, when I took them by the hand to lead them out

of Egypt — a covenant which they broke, so that I turned away from them," says Yahweh.

"But this is the covenant I shall make with the House of Israel after those days," declares Yahweh: "I shall put my law in their minds, and write it on their hearts. I will be their God, and they will be my people. No longer will they need to teach one another and tell one another to know Yahweh. For they will all know me — from the least of them to the greatest," says Yahweh. "For I shall forgive their wrongdoing, and I shall remember their sins no more." (Jeremiah 31.31-34)

How does this affect us in a personal way?

The movement from outward observance of the law to an inner one, in which we are directed by God's Spirit, is evident in the history of Israel. We often make the simplistic assumption that the Old Testament contains the old, outward law, engraved on the tablets of stone that Moses brought down from the mountain, while the New Testament contains the new covenant of the spirit. But the contrast between outer and inner law, between the law of statutes and the law of the spirit, exists in both Old and New Testaments. Jesus was the fulfilment of the new covenant, which in fact grew *in* the Old Testament, as we have seen in the course of these readings from Genesis to Ezekiel.

Our own personal journeys follow a similar route. Sometimes over and over, we follow an outward observance of the law — of civil law, of family moral codes, of church liturgies — and we learn that our journey hits a dead end unless our outward observances are transformed by an inward spiritual awareness and growth.

God gives the Holy Spirit to each one of us, at our baptism, and wants us to trust that Spirit — to trust that our inner instincts are good and right, that they come from a desire to rest in God and be at one with God's will, while our compulsions come from a need to contol what is outside us — other people, events.

If we can spend time in quiet prayer and meditation, just resting in God's love, not doing anything, we will begin to live in an *inner* harmony and perceive God's Spirit praying within us. So our prayer life must grow and develop as we become more aware of the Spirit within us. Our outward liturgies must be balanced by the prayer of quiet centring and resting in God.

Father M. Basil Pennington, a Benedictine monk, connects centring prayer with re-creation:

> In Centering Prayer we go beyond thought and image, beyond the senses and the rational mind, to that center of our being where God is working a wonderful work. There God our Father [and Mother] is not only bringing us forth at each moment in his wonderful creative love, but by virtue of the grace of filiation, which we received at baptism, he is indeed making us sons and daughters, one with his own Son, pouring out in our hearts the Spirit of his Son, so that we can in fullest sense cry, "*Abba*, Father." He says to us, in fact more than in word: "You are my son [daughter]; this day have I begotten you."[1]

Questions to Ponder

1 If you have never tried simple centring prayer, try this:

  a Find a comfortable, silent spot — in chapel or in your room. Take a comfortable position (sit, kneel), in which you will be as little aware of your posture as possible. Don't assume any posture that takes a lot of energy.

  b Be aware of the chair or pew or floor supporting you. Let your body relax into it, and picture yourself being held in God's arms.

  c Become aware of God's presence within you at the centre of your being — that place where you and God are together. Simply rest there, and enjoy being aware of God's Spirit within you. Relax and just let God love you. Don't expect to have holy feelings; this is not a method of mystical prayer to lead to transcendent experiences. It is just a simple way of giving ourselves a chance to rest in God's love.

d Some people find it helpful to choose a prayer word — a simple word or phrase that recalls God's presence. Perhaps the name "Jesus." Or "maranatha" (the Aramaic word that is used at the end of 1 Corinthians (16.22) and means "Our Lord, come"). You might repeat this word a few times, not trying to think about what it means, but just listening to it repeat itself in your soul. Whenever you find yourself distracted and your thoughts running away with you, repeat your prayer word to gently bring yourself back to an awareness of God in you.

e You will experience distractions, useless thoughts, worries, anxieties. Just let them roll over you and past you, and when you become conscious of them, bring yourself gently back to an awareness of God's presence by repeating your prayer word.

f At the end of your time (say fifteen or twenty minutes, whatever feels comfortable for you), repeat the Lord's prayer, or some other prayer, slowly, deliberately, with thanksgiving in your heart for the time you have spent with your Lord.

This kind of prayer, which needs no forms or liturgies or even words, is the most simple kind of prayer. But it's not easy, because we are so used to thinking of prayer in terms of talking to God, telling God our troubles, asking advice, confessing our sins, interceding for others. These are all important forms of prayer. And because we're so used to them, it's hard to turn off our reliance on words and just rest in God's love. But centring prayer, practised faithfully once or twice a day, morning and evening perhaps, will nourish your soul in a wonderful way.

2 Consider Psalm 42 as an expression of the longing for God that God's own being puts into our souls. It can describe the ups and downs, the hills and valleys of our spiritual journey. Reflect on this psalm, thinking of particular times in your life when you "went with the multitude and led them into the house of God" (v 4) and other times when you could only say, "why do I go so heavily while the enemy oppresses me?" (v 11) You might relate it to the map you made of your exodus journey.

3 Try writing your own psalm expressing the ups and downs of your longing for God.

4 The collect for this reading speaks of baptism as "the new covenant of reconciliation." How does that describe the prophecy from Ezekiel?

Notes

1 Basil Pennington, OSB, *Centering Prayer* (Garden City, NY: Doubleday, 1980), p. 2.

9
The Valley of Dry Bones

prophesy over these bones
prophesy to the wind
prophesy
Ezek. 37

Come, O wind, from every quarter and breathe into these dead that they may come to life. Ezek 37

The Valley of Dry Bones

The hand of Yahweh came upon me: I was carried away by the spirit of Yahweh, and set down in a valley — a valley full of bones. I was led back and forth among the bones, and I saw a great number of them spread over the valley, bones that were very dry.

Yahweh said to me, "O mortal, can these bones live again?"

I answered, "O Lord Yahweh, only you know."

Then Yahweh said to me, "Prophesy over these bones. Say to them, 'O dry bones, hear the word of Yahweh. This is the word of the Lord Yahweh to these bones: I will put breath into you, and you will live. I will fasten sinews on you, bring flesh upon you, and overlay you with skin. I will put breath into you, and you will come to life. Then you will know that I am Yahweh.'"

Then I began to prophesy as I had been commanded. And as I prophesied, there was a noise, a rattling sound, and the bones came together, bone matched to bone. As I looked, tendons and flesh appeared on them, and they were overlaid with skin. But there was no breath in them.

Then Yahweh said to me, "Prophesy to the wind; prophesy, O mortal, and say to the wind, 'The Lord Yahweh says this: Come, O wind, from every quarter and breathe into these dead, that they may come to life.'"

So I prophesied as commanded, and breath came into the bones; they came to life and stood on their feet — a vast army.

Then Yahweh said to me, "O mortal, these bones are the whole people of Israel, a people who say, 'Our bones are dry, our hope is gone; we are as good as dead.' So prophesy and say to them, 'These are the words of the Lord Yahweh: I will open your graves and lead you back to the land of Israel. When I open your graves and lift you up from them, O my people, you will know that I am Yahweh. And I will put my spirit into you and you will live; and I will set you upon your own soil. Then you will know that I, Yahweh, have spoken and have acted. It is the Lord Yahweh who speaks.'"

Ezekiel 37:1–14

1 Lord, hear my prayer,
    and in your faithfulness heed my supplications;
        answer me in your righteousness.
2 Enter not into judgement with your servant,
    for in your sight shall no one living be justified.
3 For my enemy has sought my life,
    has crushed me to the ground
        and has made me live in dark places like those who are long dead.
4 My spirit faints within me;
    my heart within me is desolate.
5 I remember the time past;
    I muse upon all your deeds;
        I consider the works of your hands.
6 I spread out my hands to you;
    my soul gasps to you like a thirsty land.
7 O Lord, make haste to answer me; my spirit fails me;
    do not hide your face from me
    or I shall be like those who go down to the Pit.
8 Let me hear of your loving-kindness in the morning,
    for I put my trust in you;
        show me the road that I must walk,
        for I lift up my soul to you.
9 Deliver me from my enemies, O Lord,
    for I flee to you for refuge.
10 Teach me to do what pleases you, for you are my God;
    let your good Spirit lead me on level ground.
11 Revive me, O Lord, for your name's sake;
    for your righteousness' sake, bring me out of trouble.
12 Of your goodness, destroy my enemies
    and bring all my foes to naught,
        for truly I am your servant.

Psalm 143

The Valley of Dry Bones

Living God,
by the Passover of your Son
you have brought us out of sin into righteousness,
and out of death into life.
Grant to those who are sealed by your Holy Spirit
the will and power to proclaim you to all the world;
through Jesus Christ our Lord. Amen.

Collect (BAS page 328)

Reflections

This is surely one of the most dramatic poetic statements in the Old Testament. It is a vision which God gave to the prophet Ezekiel, a visual promise to restore the nation of Israel to its own land, to bring them back from their "graves" in exile. But it is also a promise of God's ability and desire to resurrect the individual, as seen in a valley full of dry bones that come together as the word of God, spoken through the Lord's prophet, re-creates them. It was failure to keep God's word, the law, the covenant, that led to the exile, so the only way of salvation is by direct intervention from God, from the outside, breathing God's own Spirit into the newly remade bodies.

God's creative Spirit and God's Word are one and the same (which is of course why God is seen in the Trinity as Creator-Father, Eternal Word-Son, and Holy Spirit). So in one sense this passage is another way of getting at the truth of the previous reading — that only God's Spirit working within us can make dry bones into warm human beings whose nature is to love.

But this passage is even more dramatic because it is not just the dry and dying, but the *dead* that God can resurrect, as Jesus was raised from the dead.

The passage also tells us about prophecy. The prophet himself breathes life into the dry bones by being a vehicle for the creative Spirit.

How does this apply to us?

First, in some ways our world seems like a valley of dry bones — recall photographs you have seen of concentration camp graves, or of victims of hunger or civil war in many parts of the world. And there is certainly the potential, through nuclear war, of a worldwide valley of dry bones. But part of the prophet's message is that no matter how deeply we sin against God's creation, God can redeem it — but we must be the breath of the prophetic spirit breathing new life into a dead age. Not just heroes like Gandhi or Desmond Tutu. But we, you and I.

Second, God's word in scripture is an ever-recreating word, which can bring new life to us and, through us, to others. In the post-resurrection story about the disciples on the way to Emmaus, we see how Jesus himself opens the disciples' eyes to understand the scripture. They still do not recognize Jesus, however, until he sits down to break bread with them:

> And their eyes were opened and they recognized him; and he disappeared from their sight. Then they said to each other, "Weren't our hearts burning within us as he talked with us on the road and opened the Scriptures to us?" (Luke 24.31)

Wherever the Christian community gathers, wherever we break bread together, Jesus is there in the midst of us, saying, "you are eyewitnesses of these things" (Luke 24.48).

To listen in our hearts, in quiet reflection, to what we read on the page, is to open ourselves to endless potential for healing and new life. And to share that Word with others is to widen the potential for our own healing and that of others.

Questions to Ponder

1 When have you felt the Spirit of God breathing life into your dead body (physically, emotionally, or spiritually)?

The Valley of Dry Bones 101

2 Read the story of the disciples who meet the risen Jesus on the road to Emmaus (Luke 24.13-35) and the following collect:

> Remain with us, Lord, for the day is far spent and evening is at hand. Kindle our hearts on our way that we may recognize you in the scriptures and the breaking of bread. Grant this for the sake of your love.[1]

How do they throw light on the way God raises our dry bones to new life?

3 How might God be calling us (the church in the 1990s) and you in particular to exercise a prophetic ministry, to bring life to others? Consider the collect that accompanies this reading.

4 How does Psalm 143 remind us that God's promise to us, as to Ezekiel and the Israelites, is a promise of homecoming (their homecoming to Jerusalem, ours to a new relationship with God and our fellow creatures)? Consider especially verses 8 and 10.

5 Psalm 143 starts out as a psalm of lament, with a note of penitence in verse 2, which seems at first inappropriate for a "resurrection" reading, but of course it isn't. To "go down to the Pit" is the necessary prelude to resurrection. In the light of this penitential note, how can you make the prayer for guidance in verses 8 and 10 your own prayer of willing obedience?

Notes

1 *Book of Alternative Services*, p. 132, #13.

10
The Gathering of God's People

Shout for joy, O Daughter of Zion; exalt with all your heart. Sing for joy, YAHWEH your God in your midst is

Zeph. 3

The Gathering of God's People

Sing for joy, O daughter of Zion; and shout aloud, O Israel! Rejoice, exult with all your heart, O daughter of Jerusalem! Yahweh has repealed your sentence and has swept away your enemies. Yahweh, who rules Israel, is among you. No longer will you fear any harm. On the day of Yahweh, Jerusalem will be told this, "Have no fear, Zion. Let your hands be strong. In your midst is Yahweh your God, who is mighty to save. Yahweh will rejoice over you and be glad, will renew you by love, and will exult over you with a shout of joy, as in days long ago."

[Yahweh says:] "I will remove disaster from among you, so that none may recount your disgrace. Yes, when the time comes, I will deal with all your oppressors. I will rescue the lost and gather those who are scattered. I will transform their shame into praise and honor throughout the world. At that time, I will bring you home. At that time, I will gather you. Yes, I will make you famous and praised among all the peoples of the earth, and you will see your prosperity restored," says Yahweh.

Zephaniah 3:14–20

1 Sing to God a new song,
    for the Lord has done marvellous things.
2 With God's right hand and holy arm
    has the victory been won.
3 The Lord has made known the victory;
    God's righteousness has been openly shown in
       the sight of the nations.
4 The Lord remembers to be merciful and faithful to
       the house of Israel,
    and all the ends of the earth have seen the
       victory of our God.

5 Shout with joy to the Lord, all you lands;
    lift up your voice, rejoice, and sing.
6 Sing to the Lord with the harp,
    with the harp and the voice of song.
7 With trumpets and the sound of the horn
    shout with joy before the Lord our God.
8 Let the sea make a noise and all that is in it,
    the lands and those who dwell therein.
9 Let the rivers clap their hands,
    and let the hills ring out with joy before our God,
    when the Lord comes to judge the earth.
10 In righteousness shall God judge the world
    and the peoples with equity.

Psalm 98

O God of unchangeable power and eternal light,
look favourably on your whole Church,
that wonderful and sacred mystery.
By the effectual working of your providence,
carry out in tranquility the plan of salvation.
Let the whole world see and know
that things which were cast down are being raised up,
and things which had grown old are being made new,
and that all things are being brought to their perfection
by him through whom all things were made,
your Son Jesus Christ our Lord. Amen.

Collect (BAS page 328)

Reflections

Once again we are presented with the promise of homecoming, this time by Zephaniah, a prophet who wrote in the seventh century B.C. just before King Josiah's religious reforms began. All Israel's foes are swept away: "no longer will you fear any harm" (v 15), and "Yes, when the time comes . . . I will bring you home, I will gather you" (v 19). It recalls both the promise to Noah's family and the more all-encompassing promise in Revelation that "God will wipe away every tear from their eyes" (21.4). The late prophets' view of the restoration of Israel seems to be somewhere between an historical restoration and the eschatalogical vision of Revelation. (Considering what has happened to the Jews over the centuries, and especially in recent times, it is almost necessary to interpret this prophecy eschatologically, or as a desire of God that we humans have sabotaged.)

What does such a prophecy have to say to us, personally, living in the twentieth century after Christ?

Our "foes" are many — inner compulsions, depression, fears, selfishness, jealousies, physical limitations as well as emotional ones. At some point in our journey with God they will be cast out, and each of us will be gathered and brought home — integrated into the whole person God means us to be.

As communities and nations, we seem to have sabotaged God's plan for us to live as a human community, in harmony with each other and the rest of creation. Here, too, the prophet holds out the promise of reconciliation and wholeness.

This passage has a lot more to do with God's and our "being" than "doing" — there is no mention of a covenant or contract here, even of obedience to God's word — just an assumption of being God's people, of belonging. It prefigures Paul's vision of the reconciling love of Christ that "surpasses understanding" and that fills us "with all the fulness of God" (Ephesians 3.19).

The passage speaks to us of homecoming — coming home to our own land, both symbolically and literally. For the Israelites, land was an important part of the covenant with God and represented stability, security, and God's loving care for the chosen people. Coming home meant a renewal of the covenant and a new sense of God's loving direction.

For us, coming home to our own land may symbolically mean coming to a new acceptance of ourselves as loved by God, as belonging to God. As T.S. Eliot said,

> We shall not cease from exploration
> And the end of all our exploring
> Will be to arrive where we started
> And know the place for the first time.[1]

The place where we start is God, even before we are born:

> For you yourself created my inmost parts;
>   you knit me together in my mother's womb.
> (Psalm 139.12)

God is our home, our real native land. On our Christian journey, we have many experiences, like Dante, of wandering away from God's path, and many experiences of coming home to our own land, to our family or community, and to ourselves. To come home is to come back to our relationship with God and the Christian community and to know it in a new way, as if for the first time. It is also to come to a new or renewed understanding of our place in the wider world. The same experience that T.S. Eliot describes is pictured in slightly different imagery by St. Paul in the letter to the Ephesians:

> Bear in mind, [you who were born gentiles,] that you were once separated from Christ, excluded from the community of Israel and strangers to the covenant of promise, in a world without hope and without God. But now in Christ Jesus you who once were far off have by Christ's blood been brought near at hand. . . . Therefore you are no longer strangers and sojourners, but rather are fellow-citizens with the saints and members of God's own household — a house built on the foundation of the apostles and prophets, a house whose cornerstone is Christ Jesus himself. In Christ the whole house is fit together and grows into a holy temple in the Lord, in whom you too are being built into a dwelling place of God in the Spirit. (Ephesians 2.12-13, 19-22)

The meaning of the land, then, is centred in our hearts. We go on our journeys as pilgrims, knowing that we are at home wherever we are, whether alone or with other Christians, because as turtles carry their houses on their backs, so we carry God's love, our true home, with us. Jesus said, "foxes have dens, and birds of the air have nests, but the Chosen One has no place to lay his head" (Luke 9.58). And that is true for all of God's people.

We pilgrims tramp along on our journey with God, and coming home to our own land indicates our willingness to be open to God, our willingness to love and be loved, our willingness to take risks and make mistakes along the way, our willingness to accept our identity in relationship instead of through competitive accomplishments. And in doing that we, like Moses, might help to lead our people out of slavery, might give our world a chance to survive and become a land in which all God's creation can find fulfilment.

Questions to Ponder

1 In what ways have you experienced integration as a kind of homecoming — knowing all the scattered parts of you are brought together?

2 What enemies has God saved you from?

3 How is the Christian church a fulfilment of the promise of this prophecy? (Consider the collect that accompanies this reading).

4 Psalm 98 again suggests that God's work of salvation will extend to all the nations, which is made possible when God's salvation is no longer dependent on the keeping of the covenant law, but comes from God's direct intervention in the hearts and affairs of human beings. What is the victory referred to in verses 2–4? How does it extend to the church as well as to the people of Israel?

5 How does this extension of God's salvation to the whole world reflect the modern understanding of the mission of the church for peace and justice?

6 Using Psalm 98 as a model, write your own psalm of thanksgiving, recalling all the wonderful things God has done in your exodus journey, and asking God to help you on the rest of your journey.

Notes

1 From "Little Gidding" in the *Four Quartets, The Complete Poems and Plays 1909-1950* (New York: Harcourt Brace Jovanovich, 1971), p. 145.

Epilogue

This is our passover feast, when Christ, the true Lamb, is slain, whose blood consecrates the homes of all believers.

This is the night when Jesus Christ broke the chains of death and rose triumphant from the grave.

Night truly blessed when heaven is wedded to earth and we are reconciled with God![1]

The Great Vigil of Easter, in a dramatic way, links the Christian celebration of Christ's resurrection with the Jewish passover. The Vigil begins with the lighting of the paschal candle, symbolizing Jesus' resurrection and the new life we receive through it, and then proceeds with the singing of the Exsultet, one of the most ancient (and most beautiful) hymns of the church. The Exsultet recalls God's saving acts throughout history, identifying Jesus as the passover lamb, and culminating in his resurrection.

The paschal candle and the Exsultet provide the context in which the cycle of ten Old Testament lessons are read, and remind us, even as we are reading them, that Jesus is the fulfilment of the promises and prophecies of the Old Testament. These are followed by the Easter epistle and gospel, the renewal of baptismal vows (as well as Baptism and Confirmation if there are candidates for these sacraments), and the Easter Eucharist.

The Great Vigil of Easter has many similarities to the Jewish seder, the liturgical supper which occurs on the first night of the passover. The seder includes a service of light, a retelling of the passover story with songs and poems that celebrate the exodus from slavery, and a ceremonial meal. As in the Great Vigil of Easter, there is a dramatic narrative which connects the exodus with our own spiritual journeys:

This is a joyful but serious religious service. Its focus is the miraculous deliverance of the Children of Israel from Egyptian bondage, through peril and in the face of impossible odds, to the gifts of divine sustenance in the wilderness (the quails and manna) and of divine wisdom (the Law) at Mount Sinai — a sustenance, therefore, of the body and the soul — and at last into the freedom and beatitude of the Holy Land. This pilgrimage represents the spiritual journey from darkness into light that we all must try to make in the course of our lives.[2]

The seder ends on a note of hope. As the Haggadah (the Passover narrative) says, "the Redemption is not yet complete, and so the people of Israel are called to "the preservation and affirmation of hope."[3]

The Great Vigil of Easter ends with the Easter Eucharist, with our celebration of the presence of the risen Christ among us. And yet we, too, with the people of Israel, must respond to a call to bring hope to all people. If we go away from our glorious Easter celebration, or indeed from the Eucharist on any day of the year, to our cozy homes and the comfort of friends and families and jobs and activities, and forget all those who live without hope, we will fail in our Christian vocation.

Every seder celebration reminds the participants never to forget all that God has done for them. It is possible that the last supper, which is the basis for our Eucharist, was a seder meal (as it seems in the synoptic gospels) or else the formal meal of a leader and his followers. In either case, the importance of remembering is crucial.

It was when Israel forgot what God had done for them that they lost their way on the journey. The book of Deuteronomy is full of Moses' warnings to the Israelites to remember what God had done by leading them out of Egypt and to the threshold of the promised land, and never to forget that journey:

> Be careful to follow every commandment which I enjoin on you today, so that you may live and increase, and that you may enter and possess the land that Yahweh promised on oath to your ancestors. Remember the long way by which Yahweh

your God led you these forty years in the wilderness: to humble you and to test you by hardships, to learn what was in your hearts — whether or not you would keep the commandments of Yahweh. (Deuteronomy 8.1-2)

Every celebration of the Eucharist reminds us to remember the mighty acts of God. Every Eucharistic prayer includes a miniature history of our redemption, beginning with the creation, continuing with Christ's sacrifice, and going on into the future. Paul reminds us of the importance of remembering when he relates the institution of the Eucharist:

The tradition that I handed on to you came to me from the Lord. It is this: that on the night he was betrayed, the Lord Jesus took bread, and when he had given thanks, broke it and said, "This is my body, which is given for you. Do this for the remembrance of me." In the same way, after supper, Jesus took the cup and said, "This cup is the new covenant of my blood. Whenever you drink it, do this for the remembrance of me."

So, until the Lord comes, whenever you eat this bread and drink this cup, you are proclaiming the Lord's death. (1 Corinthians 11.23-26)

Remembering God's great love in becoming Emmanuel, God with-us, and celebrating that sacrificial love in the Eucharist, is the central act of a Christian's remembering.

We are on a journey from birth to rebirth, from creation to resurrection. And between our birth and our final resurrection are many little deaths and rebirths. Every obstacle on the journey, every problem, every broken relationship, every disappointed hope, every dream that does not come true — all of these can be given to God to be agents of growth and resurrection. We can put obstacles in the way if we resist. But God will not put obstacles there — God's way is a clear and straight path, even though it might not seem that way to us.

It is very easy to become discouraged when we look at ourselves, or at our world, because God's purpose in creation seems clearly not to have been fulfilled. The Letter to the Hebrews, however, offers us encouragement:

> Scripture says that God made the human being "ruler over all things"; this clearly includes everything. We do not, however, see humanity ruling over all things now. But we do see Jesus, who for a little while was made lower than the angels, so that through God's grace he should die for everyone. We see him now crowned with glory and honour because of the death he suffered. It was only right that God, who creates and preserves all things, should make Jesus perfect through suffering, in order to bring many sons and daughters to share his glory. For Jesus is the one who leads them to salvation. (Hebrews 2.8b–10, GNB, alt.)

While we, both communally and individually, have failed in our role as stewards over creation, God has sent Jesus to lead us to salvation, through his death and resurrection, and thereby ultimately to redeem the whole creation.

So we are brought round, full circle, from God's original creation of the world and everything in it as "very good," through our constant separation from God in our desert wanderings, through God's repeated rescues of us, through the ultimate sacrifice of Jesus on the cross and his resurrection and ascension, which made possible the coming of the Holy Spirit and God's continual recreation of us and our world.

> May the Morning Star which never sets find this flame still burning: Christ, that Morning Star, who came back from the dead, and shed his peaceful light on all creation, your Son who lives and reigns for ever and ever.[4]

Notes

1 From the Exsultet, *Book of Alternative Services*, p. 324.
2 Anthony Hecht, in Herbert Bronstein, p. 17.
3 As quoted in Herbert Bronstein, pp. 91, 93.
4 The Exsultet, *Book of Alternative Services*, p. 324.

A Note on the Great Vigil of Easter, Saturday Vigil, and Baptism

The Great Vigil of Easter

In many languages, the word for Passover and Easter are the same, *pascha*. It derives from Hebrew *pesach*, which referred to the whole drama of the Hebrew people "passing over" from slavery into freedom. The passover drama included the story of the twelve plagues and Pharaoh's stubbornness in refusing to let the Hebrews go, the eating of unleavened bread, the sacrifice of the passover lamb and smearing the blood on the lintels of the Hebrews' houses so the angel of death (who was to kill the first-born of Egypt) would pass over the houses of the Hebrews, and the climax when God led the Israelites across the Sea of Reeds into safety.

The early Christians saw in Jesus' death and resurrection a new passover in which Jesus, himself the "lamb that was slain," becomes the source of our passing over from death to life, both in a spiritual rebirth and in our eventual physical resurrection. The Great Vigil of Easter, and the Old Testament readings that are part of it, are integral to this understanding of Easter as the Christian Passover. In its double focus on Baptism and the Eucharist, the Vigil celebrates both an individual and personal passover, in which the candidate is integrated into the Christian community, and a communal passover, as the whole community participates sacramentally in Christ's death and resurrection.

The Great Vigil was celebrated at least as early as the second century A.D.[1] The earliest description of the service comes from the *Apostolic Tradition* of Hippolytus (ca 215 A.D.) and includes an all-night service of readings and instruction, with Baptism at dawn, followed by the Easter Eucharist.

As the Great Vigil evolved over the next two centuries, it came to include the lighting of the new fire and the singing of the Exsultet. By the fourth century, its structure was similar to that of the "new" liturgies of the Anglican and Roman Catholic churches, which have rediscovered the Great Vigil as the focus of the liturgical year — the central celebration of our salvation and redemption in Christ. It consisted of several parts:

1 *The Service of Light:* This included lighting the new fire, to represent Christ's resurrection from the dead and the new life we have in Christ; singing the Exsultet (from the Latin word for "rejoice") — an ancient hymn of praise recalling the passover, and connecting the Exodus event with Christ's bringing us out of slavery; and lighting and blessing the paschal candle, which was carried into the church in procession, to symbolize the pillar of cloud and pillar of fire that guided the Israelites in their exodus journey.

2 *The Liturgy of the Word:* In some places in the early church, this preceded the service of light. It began with the Old Testament readings, anywhere from four to twelve of them. Most were the same as those now in the Common Lectionary and included in this book; others sometimes included were the story of the Passover and the story of Jonah. Taken as a whole, they told the history of God's mighty acts of redemption as a prelude to the resurrection of Christ. These often took the greater part of the night, accompanied by songs and canticles and prayers. They were followed by the Epistle (usually Romans 6.3–11) and one of the Easter Gospels.

3 *Baptism and Anointing:* After the readings, at dawn (or sometimes earlier), the baptismal rite took place. Those candidates who had been preparing (often for as long as three years) and fasting (during the previous two days) were presented for baptism, in a rite that was somewhat more elaborate than our modern rites:

    a A blessing said over the "oil of thanksgiving" and an exorcism said over the "oil of exorcism."
    b The candidate renounced Satan and all evil powers and deeds, and was anointed with the oil of exorcism.

The Great Vigil of Easter, Saturday Vigil, and Baptism 117

    c The candidate was baptised by immersion, using a formula that evolved into the Apostles' Creed.

    d When the candidate emerged from the water, he or she was anointed with the oil of thanksgiving in the name of Jesus the Christ (the Anointed One) and dressed in a white robe. (The word candidate actually comes from the Latin *candidus*, meaning "white.")

    e This was followed by the laying on of hands, further anointing (this time often by the bishop), and the sign of the cross on the forehead.

4 *Celebration of the Eucharist:* The baptismal rite was followed by the Prayers of the People, the exchange of the Peace, and the Easter Eucharist. During Communion, in addition to bread and wine, the newly baptized received water (symbolizing an internal baptism) and milk & honey (symbolizing the spiritual Promised Land into which they had just entered).

The Saturday Vigil of the Resurrection

The weekly Vigil of the Resurrection developed later than the Great Vigil of Easter, but was also prevalent by the fourth century. Because the early church considered each Sunday the Lord's Day and included a celebration of the resurrection, each Saturday night came to be celebrated as a miniature version of the Easter Vigil. Its structure was similar to the structure of the Service of Light and Vigil of the Resurrection in some of the new liturgies of the Anglican and Roman Catholic churches. It included:

A Service of Light, with the singing of the ancient hymn Phos Hilaron ("O Gracious Light");

The Liturgy of the Word, with readings from both Old and New Testaments;

A Blessing over Water, a reminder of the new life we have received in Christ through our baptism, recalling the water of creation, the water through which the Israelites passed at the Exodus, the water of Jesus' baptism, and the water of our own baptism;

Conclusion: a canticle or psalm and final prayers of thanksgiving.

Christian Initiation

The rite of baptism (and later, confirmation) was intimately connected with the Great Vigil, and the water symbolism of baptism became a central symbol in the Saturday Vigil. The Christian understanding of baptism evolved from the Hebrew tradition and reflected the Christian understanding of Jesus' death and resurrection as a new passover.

Baptism in the Old Testament evolved as a way for converts to the Jewish faith to symbolically experience the Exodus and participate in the passover of Jewish history. It represented the convert's "crossing the Red Sea, entering the promised land, accepting the heritage and hopes of the Jewish people as one's own heritage and hopes."[2]

The Baptism of John in the Gospels was a symbolic washing away of the sin of the Jewish nation, the sin of the repeated broken covenants. Baptism also took on an ethical dimension, as it recognized both individual and corporate responsibility for the broken covenant. The purification of John's baptism was to allow entrance into the reformed messianic community.

The Baptism of Jesus (The Baptism of the Holy Spirit) hearkens back to Genesis and the Spirit brooding over the waters. At Jesus' baptism the Spirit once more comes down over the waters, both as an anointing (for the kingship of the Messiah and also for burial) and to establish Jesus as God's son: "You are my son, my beloved. I am well-pleased with you" (Mark 1.11). It is reminiscent of God's word proclaiming "It was very good" at each step of the creation. And it turns upside down the genealogy in Luke's gospel:

"[Jesus] was the son, so people thought, of Joseph. . ." (Luke 3.23, GNB). So the baptism of Jesus becomes the model of our baptism, of our being adopted as daughters and sons of God.

Baptism in the Early Church became a dying and rebirth into Jesus' body: "If we have been united to Christ in his death, we will certainly be united with Christ in his resurrection (Romans 6.5). Martyrs were "baptized in their own blood" as the early church saw it.

Jesus himself had connected his baptism with his death (Mark 10.38 and Matthew 20.22), and so it was natural that the early Christians should as well.

The early church also connected Christian baptism with the Exodus and with baptism in the Old Testament: "I want you to understand brothers and sisters, that our ancestors were all under the cloud, and all passed through the sea; and all were baptized into Moses in the cloud and in the sea" (1 Corinthians 10.1–2).

Baptism in the second century was very simple at first. Justin Martyr described it as both redemption from sin and initiation into the Christian church. By the end of the second century, according to Hippolytus, it had become more elaborate, part of the all-night Easter Vigil, and followed three years of preparation as well as special preparation during Lent.

Notes

1 According to Marion J. Hatchett, *Commentary on the American Prayer Book* (New York: Seabury Press, 1980), p. 240.
2 Hatchett, p. 252.

Additional Reading

Translations of the Scriptures and Commentaries

Anderson, Bernhard W. *Understanding the Old Testament*, 4th ed. Englewood Cliffs, N.J.: Prentice-Hall, Inc., 1986. A beautifully illustrated, comprehensive introduction to the history, archaeology, and literature, and theology of the Old Testament.

Boadt, Lawrence. *Reading the Old Testament: An Introduction*. New York: Paulist Press, 1984. A very clear and lively introduction to reading the Old Testament, with many helpful drawings, maps, and charts.

Craigle, Peter C. *The Old Testament: Its Background, Growth and Content.* Nashville, Abingdon Press, 1986. An easy-to-read, comprehensive survey of the Old Testament.

Hearing the Word: An Inclusive-Language Liturgical Lectionary. Washington, D.C.: St. Stephen and the Incarnation Episcopal Church, Year A, 1983; Year B, 1984; Year C, 1985. Of all the attempts to provide inclusive-language translations of the scripture, this one is the most readable. There is an interesting introduction to each of the three volumes with a helpful rationale and explanation of the process used in providing the translation. The title, *Hearing the Word*, emphasizes that the purpose is to help us hear God's word speaking to us through the words of the scripture.

Plaut, W. Gunther, ed. *The Torah: A Modern Commentary*, 1-volume edition. New York: Union of American Hebrew Congregations, 1981. One of the most helpful and comprehensive commentaries on the first five books of the Hebrew scriptures, accessible to lay people.

Books on Liturgy

Bronstein, Herbert, ed. *A Passover Haggadah*, 2nd rev. ed. Prepared by the Central Conference of American Rabbis. New York: Penguin Books, 1982. A beautifully illustrated guide to the liturgy of the Passover Seder.

Dix, Dom Gregory. *The Shape of the Liturgy*, 2nd ed. Westminster: Dacre Press, 1954. A classic and still useful study of the development of Christian liturgy, particularly the Eucharist.

Hatchett, Marion J. *Commentary on the American Prayer Book*. New York: The Seabury Press, 1980. See the sections on the Great Vigil of Easter, pp. 239–250 and on Holy Baptism, pp. 251–288.

_____, *The Sanctification of Life, Time and Space: An Introduction to Liturgical Study*. San Francisco: Harper and Row, 1976. A discussion of the origins of liturgy from the perspective of anthropology and the history of religion; provides fascinating background for Baptism and the Eucharist.

Jones, Cheslyn, Geoffrey Wainwright, & Edward Yarnold, SJ. *The Study of Liturgy*. London: SPCK, 1978. A series of articles on the development of modern liturgy based on research into the liturgy of the early church.

Knobel, Peter S., ed. *Gates of the Seasons: A Guide to the Jewish Year*. New York: Central Conference of American Rabbis. 1983. A good introduction to Jewish liturgy and its historical background.

Price, Charles, and Louis Well. *Liturgy for Living* (The Church's Teaching Series). Toronto: Anglican Book Centre. 1979. A highly readable and interesting discussion of Anglican liturgy and its background.

Talley, Thomas. *The Origins of the Liturgical Year*. New York: Pueblo Publishing Company, 1986. A readable and comprehensive, though somewhat technical, study of the historical development of Christian liturgy.

Books on Lectio Divina and Centring Prayer

Hall, Thelma, RC. *Too Deep For Words*. New York: Paulist Press, 1988. A rediscovery of the ancient monastic practice of *lectio divina*, praying with the scripture, with 500 scripture texts to use for prayer on different themes.

Keating, Thomas, OCSO. *Open Heart, Open Mind*. Warwick, NY: Amity House, 1986. A helpful book on centring prayer and its effects on inner healing; has good introductory chapters on the history and theology of contemplative prayer.

Pennington, Basil, OSB. *Centering Prayer*. Garden City, NY: Doubleday, 1980. A very helpful introduction to the subject.

Smith, Martin, SSJE. *The Word Is Very Near You*: Cambridge, Mass.: Cowley Publications. 1989. A very helpful guide to praying with the scriptures as a basis for meditative and contemplative/centring prayer. Includes many thematically arranged scriptural passages to use in prayer.

Books on Journaling and Dreams

Johnson, Robert. *Inner Work*. New York: Harper & Row. 1986. A practical guide to using dreams and active imagination for spiritual growth and healing.

Jones, Alan W. *Journey Into Christ*. New York: The Seabury Press. 1977. A sensitive and helpful guide for anyone seriously interested in the journey to wholeness.

Kelsey, Morton T. *Adventure Inward*. Minneapolis: Augsburg Publishing House, 1980. An excellent introduction to journaling as a means of spiritual growth; includes a good introduction to using dreams as a guide on our journeys.

Sanford, John A. *Dreams: God's Forgotten Language*. New York: Crossroad Publishing Company, 1980. A good introduction to dreams and the way God uses them to help us on our journeys.

Books on the Healing of Memories

Linn, Matthew, SJ, Sheila Fabricant, and Dennis Linn, SJ. *Healing the Eight Stages of Life*. New York: Paulist Press, 1974. An encouraging and helpful guide to the healing of memories throughout life's journey. One of a number of books by this team, who also offer courses on audio tapes. A comprehensive list of them is included at the end of the book.

McAll, Kenneth. *Healing the Family Tree*. London: Sheldon Press, 1984. A guide to healing those aspects of our personalities that have been inherited or affected by family dynamics — not just in our immediate families, but in previous generations as well.